Pr

"The HeartFull Way has been an extremely useful process for me and I have found it applies equally at home, on the job and in my community. The clarity it brings to conversations at work saves time and adds to everyone's sense of contribution. At home, it has helped me understand and parent my son in a new and more effective way." *—Stephanie A • Management Consultant, Mother • Canada*

"I am 16 years old and my mother has taken me to so many practitioners over the years to seek help with my anxiety and depression, including many hours of psychological counselling and medications. We feel so immensely privileged to have found Sarina. She is such a compassionate, inspiring and talented practitioner with an incredible amount of knowledge in both mainstream and alternative treatments. There has been no other person who has been able to influence my progress and healing better than Sarina. She has taught me amazing life skills which I practice every day. The technology of the HeartFull Way has gifted me a true understanding of my heart and body. My family and I will be forever grateful for Sarina." *—Molly L • Student • Australia*

"Sarina is deeply insightful and knowledgeable. Her HeartFull Way technology looks at the individual as a whole and she uses her empathic nature to get through to the issues at hand pretty accurately. Sarina will infuse you with the understanding you seek and will address the areas where you or your child/ren need to pay the most attention in order to re-ignite the optimal aliveness that may be lacking. She is formally educated in the areas that assist our children but most importantly has two grown up boys who have been her greatest teachers and it is without hesitation that I can say that if you have the privilege of working with her you can rest assured you are in excellent hands." *—Lara T • Peer Counsellor, Photographer, Mother • Canada*

"Sarina is what we are all seeking—that one person to hold our hands in taking a holistic approach to healing us and our children." *—Caron G • Business Owner, Mother • Australia*

"Full of great sorrow & heartache is how I found my way to Sarina. Using her technology (both on a conscious and somatic level) Sarina guided me in utilizing the HeartFull Way process in order to access my own inner well of wisdom and strength to move from crisis to healing."   —*Sonya N • Mother • Canada*

"The Heartfull Way process has helped me identify and peel away the stories I've been telling myself that have been perpetuating negative emotions on an on-going basis. It's created clarity where I'm able to move through emotional blocks and through this process I've actually been able to feel warmth in my heart again."
—*Jodi V • Software Sales, Mother • Canada*

"I met Sarina Auriel in October 2015 when I began her HeartFull Way program. As facilitator of our group Sarina has guided us through the deep and often confronting journey with a mix of realism, gentleness, empathy and humour.

Sarina is a safe place, she is open without judgement. Her own life experience has taught her so much. She is kind enough to share with us her many lessons."
—*Malaika S • Mother • New Zealand*

"I have been working with Sarina for about 4 months now. I am trying to learn how to communicate better with my 2 sons, 1 of whom has some special challenges with communicating himself. Sarina is patient, knowledgeable, calming and not afraid to share her invaluable personal experiences in our sessions. Sarina once called me 'braveheart' in an email to me and it had a resounding effect … she has that insight into thoughts and feelings. I am better and grateful for having met her. I look forward to continuing to work with her."
—*Nuala C • Nurse, Mother • Ireland*

The HeartFull Way

Guiding You from Surviving to Thriving

From My Heart To Yours,

Sarina Auriel

Sarina Auriel, MA CVT RYT

Redstone Publishing
2079 West 30th Ave
Vancouver, BC, Canda
V6J 3A4

www.auriel.ca

First Edition, 2016

ISBN
978-0-9952610-0-6 (paperback)
978-0-9952610-1-3 (ebook)

Jacket photo by Joshua Kier
Edited and designed by Meaghan McAneeley

To Joshy and Remey
My Heart My Soul
I love you from here to forever

ACKNOWLEDGMENTS

I would like to thank life and its many experiences for leading me on this journey. I thank my dream team of Dr. Donna Dryer, Dianna Claire Douglas, Brigitte Clark, Dr. Karen Gelmon, Dr. Myron MacDonald, Briege Farrelly, Dr. David Davis, Dr. Robin Mintzer, Gina Sunderland, Dr. Walter Lemmo and Helen Loshny. I thank my many dear and wonderful family and friends who supported me through my darkest hours so that I could reach back toward the light and share my travels with you. To note them all would take many pages, but I would like to send out a special thank you to my Australian "sisters" who always saw me as whole and my Canadian "sisters" who lent me their strength when mine faltered. I would like to thank my multidimensional guides who speak and whisper their wisdom to me every day and in every moment; my beautiful animals whose divine love sustains me; and my special park, forest and trees that speak joyous and healing words as I pass them by. I would like to thank my editor and designer Meaghan McAneeley for all her insights, patience and clear contributions to this process.

THE JOURNEY

XV   INTRODUCTION

PATH I
Preparing for Your HeartFull Way

———————————————————

I   CHAPTER 1
     Surviving Through Emotions

II   CHAPTER 2
     Don't Believe Everything You Think

19   CHAPTER 3
     From Mindful to HeartFull

27   CHAPTER 4
     The Stories We Tell

37   CHAPTER 5
     Patterns

45   CHAPTER 6
     Your Super Powers

51   CHAPTER 7
     Space, the Primary Frontier

59   CHAPTER 8
     Access Point

PATH II
Noticing the Scenery

---

69   CHAPTER 9
     Release

77   CHAPTER 10
     Here Goes the Judge

83   CHAPTER 11
     It Isn't Personal

89   CHAPTER 12
     From Confusion to Clarity

95   CHAPTER 13
     The Lights Are on
     but Nobody's Home

103 CHAPTER 14
     Distress or Stress?

111 CHAPTER 15
     The Art of Negativity

119 CHAPTER 16
     Striving Is Not Thriving

PATH III
Staying The Course

127   CHAPTER 17
Walking Side by Side

135   CHAPTER 18
Resourcing

143   CHAPTER 19
Forgiving

149   CHAPTER 20
Gifting Others with Their Journey

155   CHAPTER 21
Words

161   CHAPTER 22
The World Around You

167   CHAPTER 23
Boundaries

PATH IV
Finding Sacred Ground

177   CHAPTER 24
Connection

183   CHAPTER 25
Expansion

189   CHAPTER 26
Self-love

197   CHAPTER 27
Trust

203   CHAPTER 28
Thriving

209   POSTSCRIPT

INTRODUCTION

You are here because you are ready.... You are here because something has called you forth to this exact place and time. Something has led you to notice this book. This book is an invitation and an opportunity to move from the mind-full to the heart-full, from surviving to thriving. There came a time in my life when I realized that I had lived a very full life indeed. I began as a dancer, model and actor and was in my first world premiere production by sixteen. At nineteen I was living in Los Angeles and in my first television series. I worked both sides of the camera and became a documentary film producer and an advocate. I decided to mix my calling to create and became a union Production Designer. I taught, had children, married, divorced and switched careers, cities and countries entirely. I come from a family lineage of doctors and spiritual seekers, and so found my way back to school and got a Masters Degree in Integrated Special Education and Health. With my children in mind, I supplemented my learning by taking many varied certification programs. I have worked as a practitioner, an educator and an advocate in mind, body, spirit health and education. I work with parents and children who are having challenges in their lives and individuals going through transitions in their health and relationships.

Most of all though, I was and am a Mother. I say "most of all" because motherhood was my biggest dream. My biggest dream through all my work and my various professions was simply to be a Mom. I had my children late in life so I was ready and wanting to devote myself to enjoying being a Mom and giving from the heart. My dream changed quite rapidly when my reality became my two extraordinary children, with diverse abilities and processing issues. My vision of family changed when I found myself parenting my children as a single parent. Usually when parents are trying to describe their children to me, I get it viscerally because between the two that I have I have experienced almost everything. The impact of their diagnoses was profound. I began my career as a Mom in my heart, motivated by love and joy. I did not begin being a Mom thinking that it would be my career.

Pretty soon I began to lose track of myself, that joyful Mom, and became a firefighter. I became a hero, putting out every flame from a quick explosion to a full-scale inferno. I would be running to the school daily putting out these fires. I was still parenting from love, but joy was slowly being replaced with "have-to's" and "to-do's" and tons and tons of research. I was back at school again, researching, and there was no one around that could help. I was bringing up specialists from California and Oregon to work with my kids. At the end of each day I would beat myself up for not being in the joy, for not staying the course, for losing it or for just being too tired to rise to the occasion. I would feel shame and guilt when all I wanted was to feel joy and love.

I began looking at my children not as a gardener looks at a garden but as a mechanic looks at a car. What needed fixing, and how was I going to get it done? I became a master mechanic. Did it help them? Yes it did. But at what cost to them and to me and to our relationship as they entered their early teens. I became a leader-parent and not a supporter-parent and I was robbing my children of their most needed journey in this life. I placed my foot on the gas pedal and completely took it off the brake. I was running completely in my survival mode. I was assessing, diagnosing and coming up with a prognosis in every area of our lives—whether it was about my children or what had to get done in the day. I was very mind-full but not heart-full.

Needless to say—I woke up. But not before getting gravely ill with cancer. I woke up and realized what I always wanted to be, a whole-hearted parent. Not surviving but thriving. And I wanted the shame and judgment to stop. I wanted my children's shame and self-judgement to stop. I wanted them to move out of the anxiety they were experiencing. I wanted my kids to move out of surviving their life's experiences and into thriving in their lives. I wanted all of us to rediscover the hearts that we had abandoned for our minds. I wanted all of us to stop living a full life and move to living life fully and from our hearts.

I watched my own life come more into focus as I had the honour and privilege to see things mirrored back to me, with parents like you. Parents who did not necessarily have children with challenging needs, parents who were living their own lives in survival mode. I began to see patterns in all of us, and as I looked back I realized that for much of my life I had been what I now call "surviving the moment". I had experienced much trauma and much success, but I was surviving and not thriving. I had a very full life but my life was not being lived fully. I was not thriving. I was not really getting any of the real gifts out of my challenges. They seemed to be continually kicking me back into high gear, with my foot on my gas pedal and in surviving. I had come to the point that I was at my own growth edge. Slowly I moved from the teacher back to the student. It was this piece that would make the difference for not only myself, my health and my children, but for the work I came here to do for my clients. I made a commitment to not only discover the steps to live my life fully and out of survival, but to create the path so that I could teach others the same. The time had come to move from a very full life to a life lived very fully.

I have been working with parents such as yourself, and your children for twenty three years. I have had the honour to learn so very much from you. I learned that when you stay caught up in your mind, you over pathologize your children and your life. You begin to assess and diagnose everything in your life—from what you are going to have for dinner and why, to where you are going on holiday and what you are going to do. I learned that early trauma, that you as parents may have survived, will be passed down to your children, when you don't move into heart-fullness—and move yourself from surviving to thriving. I learned that when your children have undergone any trauma during pregnancy, labour, delivery or nursing, they are already in survival mode. When you as a loving parent experience these same traumas with your children, you and your family shift into survival mode. I learned that in this state you try to deal with the traumas from your mind, your logic, and your reason, and you still end up hitting walls. You live your life speeding forward and you feel you have no handle on anything. You live an over full life and you are barely surviving—racing from one thing to the other. I learned that you are doing the very best that you know how to do, living from your mind, but you are leaving your heart behind.

Slowly and with much compassion and love, I developed the HeartFull Way, a program that is the basis of this book. Throughout this process I bumped up against life. I experienced repeated cancer and chose to look even deeper into the notion of thriving for those going through chronic health issues. I did not want to simply survive and I knew that you did not want to either. You wanted to thrive in your life. Women are usually viscerally aware of the difference between surviving and thriving because we bear the children. We are not looking for our babies to survive only, we are looking for the signs that they are thriving. But somehow in the course of living your life, this concept of thriving has eluded you. For you, your challenges seem to be what is most in focus—what you pay attention to most. The rest of the colours in your life are less bright, your experiences less vibrant. You use the words "I have to ...." a lot. There seems to be less choice for what you are doing in any given moment. You find yourself surviving the moment. But now for the first time in years, you definitely know that you want to do things differently. You know in your bones that you are done with surviving and you are looking for a guide towards thriving.

It is my honour to now share the beginnings of the HeartFull Way in this workbook, in the hopes that you will find the guidance, and the starting point for your own journey to thriving. With this beginning, you can teach not only yourself, but your families, children, and grand-children. You can stop being a leader-parent and become a supporter-parent. You can guide your children to do their own work as you do yours. You can guide yourself to optimum health and healing,

Through my own HeartFull Way, I was able to once again look at myself and my children like I do flowers in a garden. I asked myself what the soil was needing, how the water quality and the food was? I asked myself whether each flower needed to be moved or have more sunshine or less sunshine? I left being a mechanic behind. I learned how to trust our connection to heart. We became heart-full. My children were able to develop their own faith and confidence in their growth curve. They were able to connect to their heart to know what was needed in the moment, and what they could request for them-selves. They found their witness and their choices in their own heart. They felt encouraged and enlivened again within their thriving and got to feel whole and complete. Through the HeartFull Way we all thrived.

I invite you now to walk step-by-step on this journey with me. Become aware of the beauty and sanctity of your own travels. I invite you to experience the bones of my HeartFull Way program and help to model a new way of being for your children. I invite you to read, explore, discover and play your way through this journey. The book is divided into four paths. In **Path I, "Preparing For Your HeartFull Way"**, you will find your heart again, discover your witness and learn all the foundational principles that you will use on your journey. You will explore the default position that you are inhabiting within survival mode, called your Picasso Response. You will learn to move into an Aligned Response and finally a HeartFull Response. You will move from mind-full to heart-full. **In Path II** of your pilgrimage, **"Noticing the Scenery"**, you will transform much of how you have been experiencing your life. You will learn how to become aware and notice, so you can move forward on your journey. You will discover the power in releasing the patterns and course correcting for the remainder of your journey. **In Path III, "Staying The Course"**, you will move to transmute that which you experienced personally and inside yourself, to a place that is not personal and outside yourself. Your past traumas will have been transformed in quality and now become transmuted so that they no longer determine your future. In **Path IV** of your travels, **"Finding Sacred Ground"**, you will transcend your past traumas and responses and find the sacred ground that your new life will be built upon.

Each chapter has an invitation to a practice to assist you on this journey. You will discover your three brains of mind, belly and heart. You will practice how to move into and out of each and how to use your breath. There is room to reflect and journal right in the book. Know that if this does not serve you, and you need more space to write and record, I invite you to buy yourself a journal that feels wonderful in your hands to keep track of your HeartFull Way. These practices are for you to play with and discover for yourself.

May you fall in love with your life and may you begin to truly live your life fully.

From my heart to yours,

Sarina Auriel

PATH I

Preparing for Your HeartFull Way

CHAPTER I
Surviving Through Emotions

CONGRATULATIONS! I BET YOU DIDN'T EXPECT ME TO SAY THAT. YOU are surviving. You have already taken a major step on your HeartFull Way towards thriving. You have been through the phase of suffering and victimhood and have survived. How do I know this to be true for you? Suffering is when you believe that life is something that is happening to you rather than something you are creating. Suffering is when you are scared to death to be here on this planet under the effects of life. When you are afraid to be present in any way. When you dread the concept of really living, and are unwilling to commit to any journey towards healing. When you are in victimhood and suffering, your life is small and constricted. I know that you are now surviving, not suffering, because if you were in your victimhood phase you would not have found this book or entertained this HeartFull Way.

Now that you are surviving, you are out in the world and yet every time you seem to gain traction in your life, you hit a boulder or a dead end. You may experience these setbacks on a mental, physical or spiritual level. You understand that there is a different way to embark on a healing journey, and your are looking for the right guide.

Most people who are surviving have been through some kind of trauma, pain or dysfunction in their lives. The experienced trauma does not need to have been immense yet it might have been life altering. It might be that you never felt heard as a child or that you have gone through cancer. In other words it might be considered developmental trauma or it might be considered shock trauma. It might be the trauma of a dysfunctional relationship, or the trauma of experiencing physical or spiritual pain. Trauma is an experience that you could not handle at the time and so the range of what it could be is huge. Whatever trauma you have experienced, take a moment, pat yourself on the back and realize that you did the best you could with the tools that you had. You climbed out of the hole of suffering or victimhood and you are surviving. You have survived and you are here looking forward to this book as the guide for your healing journey to thriving. You know deep inside your bones that you wish to thrive. You may not even know what thriving is or what it will look like but you are taking steps towards that place. The proof is that you are here beginning your HeartFull Way.

Usually it is when you hit obstacles in your journey that you begin to realize that you are still surviving and not thriving. You sense that you have left your suffering behind you in the dust of your life's path, because you can feel your own movement forward, and yet you are still finding boulders and rocks, instead of new routes and tracks. Patterns begin to emerge and repeat. Chronic illness may surface, anxieties may begin or you may have trouble sleeping. You begin to feel dissatisfied but don't necessarily know the cause of it. You try a new hobby or even a new relationship, but it doesn't really change things at the heart of it all. What you feel and what you think are not often in sync, and you rarely feel heart-full. There is no magical age at which this happens. This back and forth between sufferer and survivor can also keep repeating until you firmly commit to your pilgrimage. Until the boulders you hit are simply too hard to withstand any longer, the experiences too life shifting, and you are no longer willing to live a life that is half full.

Surviving was the path you took out of suffering. It is how you got here but not where you want to stay and live for the rest of your life. You want to move from living this very full life to living your life fully and in the present moment. You can do so by committing to this healing journey—this HeartFull Way. Under the guidance of this book you can learn to thrive.

To begin your HeartFull Way I am going to guide you in identifying your emotions, locating your thoughts, and moving into your heart. So before you journey onward, it is important to notice how you experience the emotions of surviving. Your emotions are located in your belly. Your belly is where your enteric brain exists. Your belly contains millions of neurons. It is your second brain. Some of the emotions that are stored in your belly are carried over form your suffering or victimhood period. Some of these emotions may now be experienced as anxiety or anger. They may be experienced as fatigue or illness. They may be experienced as disconnection or loss. Some of these emotions have been carried around since the original trauma, pain or dysfunction took place. Understand that your emotions are imprinted on you and in you until you become aware of them. This is what is known as cellular memory. It is your body's memories stored as emotions. These emotional memories are as automatic as your breathing. Until of course they are not. And that is where you begin your HeartFull Way—with an exercise to help you to become aware.

Take a moment to imagine that you have three balloons. One in your head, representing your thoughts, one in your heart, representing coherence, and one in your belly, representing emotions. Think of a time when you felt overwhelmed by your emotions. Perhaps when you were tired and became frustrated with your child, or when you had an argument with your best friend, or when a relationship ended for you. Close your eyes and notice how the memory feels. This is a place of triggered emotions. An event occurred and your imprinted emotions have been triggered or stimulated into play.

Check in with your body. It might feel like your balloons just blew away. It might feel like your mind is going to the right and your belly to the left. Your heart might feel sunken. I call this the Picasso Response. Picasso is well known for paintings where parts of the body are disconnected, painted at odd angles, floating in space. If you were to paint yourself right now it would be like a Picasso. You would paint your head on one side, your chest in the middle and your belly to the other side. All these vital parts of yourself would be floating in space, disconnected from one another. Stay with your Picasso Response for a couple of moments if you can. It is very important to be able to identify what your Picasso Response feels like, so that you can recognize it moment by moment in your life.

Emotions can be translated to energy in motion. Dr. Jill Bolte Taylor states that emotions are meant to only last ninety seconds in the body. I believe they are meant to come up, give you a message that things are either working for you or not and move out. You will see this with your young children if their emotions have not been thwarted at an early age. One minute they are giggling, the next they are crying, the next they are filled with wonder. Each emotion runs through them letting them know what is or isn't working for them in their environment and experiences.

After experiencing the message of an emotion, the body is then meant to adjust and move towards or away from the situation that stimulated the emotion. As a person in survival, this won't be your experience. Through your experiences of trauma, your energy-in-motion got stuck. It might have been that at one time you could not move away from a dysfunctional situation and you became stuck there. If you were a child dependent on parents for your survival and yet those parents were causing your trauma, you would not have been able to physically move away from the situation. And if the only motion that you are now experiencing is your body moving into a Picasso Response, you will indeed see the same results showing up in your life again and again. Your emotions, rather than being an energy that moved up and out, got squashed down somewhere in the body. Yet these emotions still retain their energy and they want to move. So at the most inappropriate times they may bubble up. They replay bit by bit as you lash out at those you love or find yourself crying with minimum provocation.

Your original emotions may also have been layered over by another set of emotions designed to help you move from your suffering to surviving. I call this layering, one emotion covered by another, an emotional sandwich. If you were bullied at school you may have felt terrified. If you were unable to express this emotion and move away from those who caused you to feel this way, you may then have adopted two more layers of emotion. You may have a layer of shame about the kind of person you are—about being the kind of person that this could happen to. Or you might have thought that you should have fought back. Then you'd have added a layer of detachment, so that you could say to yourself, "I don't care, it doesn't bother me." The result is three layers of emotion, an emotional sandwich with shame at its centre. What are the emotions that seem to bubble up out of nowhere for you? What are the emotions that you keep repeating to yourself and expressing to your friends? What are the emotions you keep replaying and rethinking? It is like putting the same song on again and again, replaying an event and creating the same emotions. Notice the different kinds of emotions that may be living in you. Emotions that were never allowed to be expressed in the moment, emotions that you have been hiding from and emotions that have now gotten stuck in a groove that at one time helped you to survive. Emotions that allowed you to move away from your pain. When in survival experiencing recurring emotions, you are either stuffing these emotions down further or rebooting them, rather than allowing them to move and to release. These emotions are being replayed for a purpose. They helped you to survive the unthinkable for yourself. They helped you to survive what would have been too much for you at the time.

I recently saw this emotional sandwiching play out very clearly with a young client of mine. Her parents had moved her away from what was familiar. The family moved to another country, city, school and environment. She had no input into the decision. She had no control over her life. She was so very heartbroken. Her parents thought that the best way to deal with all this was to always look on the bright side and have a sunny disposition. There was no guidance to help her to express her authentic emotions. In order to survive the grief and loss that she was not equipped to feel and experience by herself, she made herself a sandwich, first feeling great shame for feeling her grief and then adding anger for her top layer. The anger became her go to emotion, and the only one that people took notice of because it was disruptive to them. These were the emotions that she chose to help her to survive the unthinkable. They were also emotions that were constantly placing her in her Picasso Response. Unfortunately from the Picasso Response she could not access her real feelings or make choices that worked for her.

You are a bright and talented star to have developed the ability to move past your suffering and into surviving by using your very own particular emotions, and creating your very own particular emotional sandwiches. Your emotions helped you to move away from your trauma. Take a moment to acknowledge yourself for that. And now it is time to move on. To slowly and lovingly take the first steps on your way out of surviving, and prepare yourself for your HeartFull Way to thriving. You begin to prepare by identifying all of these types of emotions and by learning to recognize that the way you have been experiencing them places you in your Picasso Response.

Invitation

I invite you to find a safe and comfy place where you might want to spend your time doing the Invitations that you will find throughout this book. You might choose an indoor space or an outdoor space. You are going to begin your HeartFull Way by finding this exterior physical space. Now let that safe comfy place also find its way to inhabit your body, so that the way you are sitting, resting or reclining in your body feels safe and comfy to you. Take a few breaths and see if you can find your breathing both safe and comfy. Notice the quality of the breath that you are starting with and see if you can connect to that breath, finding its pattern, its constancy. When you feel settled and safe in your body, I invite you to think about a triggering emotion that came up for you more than once this week. An emotion that was the stimulus for sending you into your Picasso Response. What emotions came up for you during your day? What emotions are coming up for you right now?

Most people who are in the survival stage only have a few emotions that they can name because most of the time they are replaying the same ones. These are usually the emotions that they have layered over their original pain. There is nothing to change or to fix about what you find, simply be the ever curious observer and notice. Notice if you feel out of alignment and in your Picasso Response as you turn your attention to the emotions you are replaying. See if you can connect to your Picasso Response. What is your body doing while going through the Picasso Response? What is happening to your three balloons? What do you and your heart rate feel like? Notice if the emotions trigger your body to feel like the event is happening again in the here and now. Take at least five to ten breaths exploring and getting to know your very own private Picasso Response. Then begin to breathe in, hold the breath at the top, where your in breath ends, for a count of three and then release the breath with a long sigh. Repeat until you feel centred once more. Then bring some gentle movement to your head, your hands and your feet.

Write down what your Picasso Response felt like. Throughout the week, I would like to invite you to notice the emotions that trigger your Picasso Response and keep a record of them in the space provided below. Observe if these emotions are repeating emotions. If you are having trouble with identifying names for your emotions, I suggest you search the internet for a list of feelings. The best lists that I have found are from the Centre for Nonviolent Communication, www.cnv.org. Enjoy the amazing self that you are. Enjoy discovering how you have used your emotions to survive.

CHAPTER 2

Don't Believe Everything You Think

YOUR MIND IS FULL OF YOUR THOUGHTS. YOUR MIND IS FULL OF rationality and logic. But despite your capability for linear rational thought, you as a human don't function best that way. As discussed in Chapter 1, "Surviving Through Emotions", an event may trigger you or cause you to relive emotions, transporting you to a previous time and place. Anytime you are triggered, you abandon your creative right brain. You are left with only a working left brain, which is not a great place to be. The left brain is not equipped to problem solve, think outside the box or create new and amazing life possibilities for you. When left alone, this beautiful half mind of yours, your left brain, then loops on thoughts, sticking you to what you think you know in the moment. What you think you know while only using a small portion of your brain—unable to use your full capacity. Your left brain also finds it very difficult to take on another person's perspective. It doesn't think in the abstract. It only recognizes the concrete past of your life experiences. When you are triggered or stimulated, you are living from this half brain. You don't have the advantage of your whole brain working. Take a moment now and simply sit with this.

Some of you who are parents will recognize this place of half brain in your children. Something happens to them that traumatizes their "new in the world" selves, their beginners in life selves. They don't have the skills or the tools to deal with the new situation they are presented with, so they let go and "lose it". You sweep in trying to speak to them, calm them, distract them, solve their problem for them, and they will have none of it. They have no access to the part of their brain that could do any of the above. I remember the first time I lost it when I was a child. I did not have the tools to deal with the large emotions that I was feeling and my mother had no tools to be a container, a holder of space for me. She was way too uncomfortable with my emotions. She walked away stating that she could not deal with me if I was going to be that emotional. I remember where I was, what it looked like, and even the smell in the house. That experience, or what we might call that trauma, got so locked into me, that it changed the way I experienced emotions. From then on, instead of letting an emotion flow through me in a healthy manner, I would immediately go into a Picasso Response, go into my half brain and think through the emotions, rather than feeling them and processing them. I did this over and over again in order to retain a connection with my mother and then later because it was my learned way to survive. You have these experiences as well. You have your own way that you used your thoughts to survive.

In Chapter 1, you looked at how your body has held onto emotions that come up repeatedly to help you move from suffering to surviving. As your body carries these past linked emotions your mind carries these past linked thoughts. This is how you survived. Now let's revisit the Invitation from Chapter 1: what was one time you discovered that you became triggered and found yourself in your Picasso Response? In that moment you didn't have access to your emotions. Instead your emotions pulled your belly out to the right, beginning your Picasso Response. What happened next was that your half brain wanted to make sense of it all, so it began to pull your mind out to the left, increasing this Picasso Response. With your belly to the left and your mind to the right, you experienced your emotions as factual thought. If someone were to ask you how you were feeling in this triggered Picasso Response moment, with half your brain off and using your emotions to think, you would probably answer them with one of your few basic emotions, sad, angry or frustrated. These are the few basic emotions that you have learned from childhood experiences.

The rest of your answer would not have to do with how you are feeling emotionally. You would be retelling the story of what happened or what you were thinking about what happened. It might go something like this. You meet your friend for tea and they see that something is wrong. They ask you how you are feeling. Your response is, " I called my doctor when I was supposed to and it constantly went to voicemail, no matter how often I dialled. Why would they even ask me to call them at that time? How insulting. What a waste of my time. It makes me so angry." The emotion here is being thought about, not actually felt. You are thinking that you are angry but perhaps you are frustrated, or hurt, or disappointed. There is no way of knowing because you are stuck in Picasso Response with both your thoughts and your emotions. Your friend only gets the story, and your thinking emotions.

When you are in survival, you are constantly replaying both thoughts and emotions, thoughts and emotions, thoughts and emotions. Your Picasso Response leads you into same time, same channel mode without any access to your whole creative brain. By replaying thoughts and emotions you have been training your beautiful self to survive, which is an amazing accomplishment. You have also been training your entire being to think emotions in the same way over and over again. When you think your emotions you hold on to them rather than allowing them to flow through you. When you entrench your thoughts from a place of Picasso Response you also hold fast to your place in time, without any hope of being able to truly prepare for your healing journey. For now, notice how often you think your emotions. Be kind and gentle here as your HeartFull Way is only at the preparation stage. Remember, being in your Picasso Response allowed you to survive and brought you to this moment.

In order to prepare you for your journey, this book will guide you to move from your Picasso Response into your Aligned Response. Later you will learn to move from your Aligned Response to your HeartFull Response, one step at a time. In this week's Invitation you will take your next steps of preparation by discovering and becoming your Aligned Response.

Invitation

I invite you to go back to your safe and comfy place. You may use pillows, bolsters or blankets to support your body—whatever makes you feel safe. Now let that safe place find its way into your body. Take a few breaths and see if you can find this feeling of safety inside. Notice the quality of the breath that you are starting with here and see if you can connect to that breath. Where does that breath begin and where does that breath end? Is it loose or tight, gentle or strong? When you feel settled and safe in your body, locate your mind, your heart and your belly. Imagine your three balloons: in your mind, in the centre of your chest and in your belly, all stacked perfectly, one on top of the other, separated from each other by a golden cord. Allow this golden cord to originate well above your head. Let it travel down and attach to your mind balloon at the back of the balloon, travel down further and attach to your heart balloon, and finally travel down and attach to your belly balloon. Allow this golden cord to end well below your belly balloon in the deep earth. Breathe here and notice how it feels to be in alignment, with your mind, heart and belly all lined up. Take a few additional breaths here. This is your Aligned Response.

It is time to play a bit. Imagine an experience that you had this past week, that placed you in your Picasso Response. Watch your body relive this moment and allow yourself to experience your Picasso Response again. Feel that and recognize your Picasso Response as a heads up. Slowly acknowledge your Picasso Response, and thank it for letting you know that it is time to move into your Aligned Response. Now slowly line up your balloons, mind, heart and belly, with your golden thread joining them together. Breathe here in your Aligned Response for five to ten more breaths. When you feel complete in this place of Aligned Response you may begin to come back to your surroundings, move hands and feet and open your eyes.

I invite you to write down two times that you were able to move into your Aligned Response this week. Two times that you were able to realign out of your Picasso Response, with all pieces going this way and that, to an Aligned Response, where your mind, the place where your thoughts live, your heart, the place where your love lives, and your belly, the place where your emotions live, are all lined up in a straight line. What helped you get realigned? What worked for you? How can you make this journey, to Aligned Response, more often?

output:

CHAPTER 3
From Mindful to HeartFull

YOU ARE HERE BECAUSE YOU ARE READY. READY TO MOVE INTO THE deep parts of yourself to prepare for your HeartFull Way. Ready to take the journey from mind-full or emotion-full to heart-full. Ready to stretch and strengthen that heart-full connection to yourself so you are prepared when the road might get rocky or hilly.

Like a musician who has an instrument to play, you have your body in which to travel on this path. Let's begin this chapter with looking at the heart at the centre of your body. It is no accident that your heart has been placed between your mind and your belly. Between what produces your thoughts and what produces your emotions. Your heart is your unique gift, strategically placed, with its purpose being to navigate, vibrate and generate anything that you produce with thought or emotion. Most of the time you are not conscious of this miraculous tool that you have. You see your heart either from a medical point of view or a romantic point of view. Dr. Armour's research revealed that the heart has over forty thousand neurons. The heart can think, remember and learn all on its own. The heart is your third brain.

I invite you today to see your heart as your guidance or navigation system and your generator. Your heart guides, navigates and generates by its natural power of love. Your heart navigates as it turns thoughts into wisdom and emotions into understanding. It then generates those clear and present vibrations of wisdom and understanding out into the world. If your heart is hooked up to an Aligned Response, then your emotions, rather than flying all over the place, can be turned into internal understanding with the heart's guidance, and can be given more life force and energy vibrations by the heart's generator. If you are in your Aligned Response, the thoughts you have can be navigated into wisdom and energized to help you to produce your very own creations. Your heart is your very own guide and generator to assist you on your journey from surviving to thriving.

To do this your heart must move from Aligned Response to HeartFull Response. HeartFull Response is your very own holy trinity, thoughts and emotions processed through the loving heart. The heart has the ability to send radio-like waves into your life and into your entire life's time capsule of past, present and future. Those radio waves, when originating from your Aligned Response and ending in your HeartFull Response, can be clear and help you to meet your purpose. Or, when you are in your Picasso Response, those waves can falter, and you are back into surviving once more.

So take a moment to notice how this all works. Find your three balloons from Chapter 1, "Surviving Through Emotions". This time however, try imagining them as pearls. Think of a time when your mind and your emotions were aligned, not triggered or scattered, not in your Picasso Response. This could have been when you were celebrating a new job that you really worked hard to get, when getting a new puppy or kitten, or when you were holding your newborn. Whatever event you pick, close your eyes and allow yourself to be right in the event. Notice the feeling. From this place you immediately go into your Aligned Response. All three pearls line up, one on top of the other. You then naturally begin to move your pearls: your thoughts move down into your heart at the same time that your emotions come up to your heart. You are in your holy trinity. You may begin to feel as though your heart is growing as big as the room and beyond (we will get into this next step later). You can feel your heart generating joy and connection. Stay with that feeling for a couple of moments and notice that you are in fact feeling, and are no longer thinking emotions. You are full of your heart or heart-full. I call this your HeartFull Response. All three pearls are in your heart space together in the middle of your chest. Continue to notice the pulse of your heart out into the world around you. This is your heart generating your vibrations. How does your breath feel right now? Imagine what people would be feeling in your presence, or as they passed you on the street.

In the last two chapters you explored the emotions of survival and the survival habit of thinking emotions. Survival mode is characterized by the Picasso Response, where thoughts and emotions are scattered in all directions. The Picasso Response is where you think your emotions without having access to feeling, understanding or wisdom. Feeling, understanding and wisdom comes from being first in an Aligned Response and then moving into a HeartFull Response. In Picasso Response you have no access to your feeling because it is in your heart that you can understand and connect to feeling. In Picasso Response you have no access to your wisdom because it is in your heart that knowledge turns into wisdom. When you are not in your HeartFull Response you can only react, you can't create. Your HeartFull Response takes you one step further than an Aligned Response. If you were to simply stay in an Aligned Response you could be pulled back into a Picasso Response by being triggered by a thought or an emotion. When you set upon your journey from your HeartFull Response you fully integrate the self that you are, the self of thoughts and the self of emotions, and you become present to yourself within your here-and-now body. This here-and-now body is the integrated body that can make the journey from surviving to thriving through your HeartFull Way.

Now look at the same situation you looked at in Chapter 1. Perhaps the one where you were frustrated with your child. You have the option of staying in a triggered Picasso Response where you say to yourself, "He is letting me down"—but that's not a very empowered place. No great radio waves being put out into your world. You can, however, make another choice to move into your Aligned Response and then step into your HeartFull Response, where you remember what a wonderful gift it was to have this child. Let your heart grow large. Through the wise and understanding place of your heart, you can hold the space and create the requests that lead to solutions for your family. You can find your needs with your heart and create the requests for what it is you need moment by moment. You can create your own heart-full solutions. Your heart can do this—it can send out these new amazing radio waves and vibrations. What a powerful way to live your life.

Many programs discuss mindfulness and its various benefits. I believe that the term mindfulness has become outdated. It is part of the last millennium. It is part of the generations that were both suffering and surviving, and looking for a way out of their feelings. It is a concept that deals with a stillness of the mind, but it does not integrate the whole self or help you to use the power of the heart. You will hear individuals speaking about mindfulness with words that still evaluate. Words that evaluate a good and perfect state. Mindfulness focusses on the very place that you are stuck, your head, where your thoughts are creating your issues. However, it is not only thoughts that create your issues. It is the combination of your thoughts fired up by your emotions. You can't think yourself out of your emotions. Mindfulness is a wonderful place to begin to be in contact with the mind and thoughts, but it has forsaken the emotions, and how to best move both thoughts and emotions into the heart. It is my belief that mindfulness falls short of what is needed for us in this millennium. You need more to move past this legacy of evaluation and the mind, and into your own legacy of the heart, the legacy which you will wish to pass on to your children. So I invite you to move from mindfulness to heart-fullness as individuals and communities. To allow your heart, this miraculous vibrational guidance system and generator, to help you to create a life lived fully and with heart. Your heart is the place where a new type of energy can solve problems because they were not created from or by the heart, but rather they were created by thought or by emotion. This is a most powerful place to inhabit and come into relationship with. Continue with your HeartFull Way and journey into a life of thriving in the present and dancing into a future of your choosing and creation.

Invitation

I invite you to find to your comfy place once more—with pillows, bolsters or blankets if you like. Notice the quality of the breath that you are starting with here and see if you can connect to that breath. Take a moment now and adjust yourself or your props in whatever way will make you feel safe. Now let that safe place find its way into your body. Take a few breaths and see if you can find this feeling of safety inside you. Once you have found this feeling, notice if the quality of your breath has shifted from the way it was when you sat or laid down. When you feel settled and safe in your body, locate your mind, your heart and your belly—your three pearls. Take a few breaths here. Imagine your mind, heart and belly all stacked perfectly one on top of the other, joined together by a golden string—this is your Aligned Response. Some of my clients prefer three flowers. Find the image that will work for you. You are now going to step forward from your Aligned Response to your HeartFull Response.

Visualize your mind, heart and belly pearls as three colours. Are they all different colours or are they the same colour for you? Bring your awareness to your mind pearl and slowly let it move and slide down into your heart space. Notice if the colours of these two pearls change as they merge together. Take your time. Breathe. Connect with your belly pearl and slowly let it slide up to your heart space as well. Notice if the colour or shape of your new, single pearl changes again as your holy trinity of mind, belly and heart become one. This is your HeartFull Response. Take three to five breaths here in your HeartFull Response. See your heart pearl expanding with each breath. Feel what this feels like for you. Notice how it feels to experience life from here. Enjoy your time here for as long as it suits you. When you feel complete bring your awareness to your hands and feet, fingers and toes. Wiggle them and bring gentle

*movement into your body by dropping your chin to your chest
and letting it rock forward from side to side. Open your eyes
and make a note of your experience. This week I invite you to
come into your HeartFull Response when you wake up every
morning and before you go to bed every night.*

*This experience of feeling what it is to be heart-full, is the
pivotal step to prepare for your HeartFull Way, so you can travel
from surviving to thriving. Practice by simply becoming aware
or noticing the moments you are aligned and in HeartFull
Response, taking the beat, the breath, to welcome heart-full,
and then beginning to create more of these HeartFull Response
moments. Every time you feel misaligned, every time you feel
all in your mind or all in your emotions, stop, take a breath.
See what you need to do to line up the thought and the emotion
with the understanding, the mind and the belly with the heart.
Then come into your HeartFull Response and take three to five
quiet breaths. I invite you to write down two times that you
were able to move into HeartFull Response this week. Then
notice how life shows up.*

CHAPTER 4
The Stories We Tell

IN THE PAST FEW CHAPTERS YOU BEGAN YOUR PREPARATIONS FOR your HeartFull Way to thriving. You moved from your Picasso Response, to your Aligned Response and then into your miraculous HeartFull Response. Such wonderful preparations. Before you take off fully on your own path, you need to be realistic about things that can happen on any journey. You might stumble on a hole in the road or find a boulder in your way, or you might even take the wrong turn and need to go back. In this chapter you are going to explore one of the stumbling blocks that you might encounter on your HeartFull Way, and what the impact might be on you and your journey.

You are an amazing writer and story teller. You have told yourself so many stories in order to survive. You have now learned that your emotions or your thoughts can pull you back into your Picasso Response. The stories you repeat to yourself and others can do this too. A story is when you have linked your thoughts and emotions together to create a narrative.

Here is an example. I remember needing to switch doctors because my doctor had moved away. Instead of reading my file, the new doctor asked me to tell them what had been happening for me over the past couple of years. The story I retold was a combination of all the thoughts and emotions that I had experienced during the past years of cancer treatments. I left the office not healed but extremely agitated.

Because I was required to retell the story, I also relived the story in my body. My body was pulled back into Picasso Response and my cells could not tell the difference between the story I told on this day, and the actual events that happened two years ago. Stories keep Picasso Response activated in your body. Stories attach themselves to very specific emotions and thoughts. Together stories, thoughts and emotions lead your body to repeat the same reactions in a dramatic loop impacting your life and your ability to thrive.

Emotions on their own are life affirming and informative. As I said before, emotions are your energy in motion (e+motion), letting you know in the moment what you are being asked to pay attention to. Thoughts without attachment to story are observations rather than evaluations. They come in, you notice, you receive the message, you go into your Aligned Response (mind, heart, belly) then your HeartFull Response (all pearls in your heart). You expand in this heart-full place. The love that your heart feeds your thoughts and emotions allows the wisdom and understanding to arise and you get to move on with your thriving. Easy, right? Wrong.

For the person caught in the loop of survival, stories can be your trap—your pitfall. For example, consider the pure emotion of anger. You observed something in your environment that was not working for you. This thought or observation led to an emotion of anger. In anger there is no story—only an observation. Anger is an emotional messenger that brings you to attention through heat and through discomfort. In its pure form, it is a real messenger that is teaching you about yourself and your world. It is saying "Some need of mine is not being met. Pay attention please." However, if you take this beautiful, pure, authentic messenger, and you add your once-upon-a-time story to it, you end up with rage. Rage is not anger. Rage is the emotion of anger plus a story. Where anger informs and creates space for you to investigate this moment, rage wreaks havoc on you and causes maximum drama and destruction in your life.

I am going to walk you through a very simple example of this phenomenon. Say you are a parent of two teenagers. You spend your time being a very attentive mother. You have had the flu for the past two days and have barely lifted your head off the pillow. Day three comes around and you feel well enough to wander into the kitchen. The kitchens dirty dishes and used pots and pans on most of the surfaces. This is your observation or your thought. The first emotion that comes up for you is anger. That anger is telling you that something in your environment is not a fit. You don't know yet what that is as your body is simply experiencing the emotion and the thought as separate pieces. Then before you can align and get into your HeartFull Response, your story begins. It might go something like this: "I can't believe this. These kids are so thoughtless. They don't care about me. They don't respect me. I don't matter." I think you get the picture. Pretty soon that anger becomes rage and you can't wait to get your hands on those kids and give them a loud piece of your mind. That is the drama that you will bring into your life when you live from a Picasso Response. Was it true that the kitchen was in a state of disarray? Yes it was. The kitchen in a state of disarray is a thought as anger is an emotion. But everything else was a story. Most of the time teenagers aren't so much thought-less as thought-full. They are so very full of their own thoughts going a mile a minute, thinking of this and that. Thinking of themselves and their friends and their own activities and needs.

Now let's examine the same scenario from the perspective of your HeartFull Response with no story involved. You come into the kitchen and see the same scene. Your thought is that the kitchen has dishes on every surface. This time you feel the emotion of anger coming up. You sense your story beginning. You stop, go into an Aligned Response, recognize your mind, heart and belly, and then bring your balloons into your heart. You are now in HeartFull Response and from here you can figure out which of your values is not being honoured in this situation. Perhaps you value consideration or community cooperation. From here you remember that part of parenting is also preparing your kids. You realize that you need to make a very clear request so they are prepared to behave in a different way when this kind of situation comes up again in their lives. Perhaps it will come up again with you or perhaps with their spouse when they are older. There is no drama and your story has not taken you into survival. You are able to be clear and continue on your journey.

Your stories will not only change your emotional messengers, as you saw from an emotional messenger of anger transforming into an emotional messenger of rage, they will also pull you into your old familiar patterns. I'll explain more about patterns in the next chapter. Even if you don't begin with any particular emotion or thought, by constantly being absorbed in your stories and retelling them over and over again, you will keep yourself in Picasso Response and in survival mode. Your stories will become the matter and the fibre in your life and keep you surviving rather than thriving. I see this a lot in my clients who have had an illness at one time or another. They never quite get to feeling well because they are always telling their story. The story pulls their mind to the left, where a thought or observation quickly turns into an evaluation. This then sparks their emotions and brings their belly to the right, placing them yet again in Picasso Response. The cells never get a chance to experience a HeartFull Response and full wellness.

I want to be clear here. I don't mean to say that the stories did not happen at all or did not happen in some form. The truth is they probably did, somewhere, and at some time. You might be a parent who has a child with some special need. This is true. It becomes a story when it is repeated over and over again, when you begin to identify with the story, and when the story begins to run your emotions, your thoughts and then your life. In fact, the repetition of your story, combined with the strength of the new emotions the story produces and the vibrations that they create together, makes it nearly impossible for you or your family to shift and grow through and past your child's diagnosis. You saw in the last chapter how your heart is a strong generator of vibrations. Depending on which response you find yourself in, whether it is a Picasso Response, an Aligned Response or a HeartFull Response, the quality of the vibrations you experience within yourself and project out into the world, is either positive or negative.

I have worked with young adults who had various learning challenges while in their early developmental years. When tested, these young adults no longer demonstrate the same issues, but the story of their past challenges coupled with the strength of their own heart's generator allows the continuation of their learning issues to show up in the here and now. For these young adults there is comfort in the sameness of their situation. There is comfort in surviving even if there is no thriving.

Just imagine what emotions and thoughts would come up if you told the following story over and over again: the story of how you're tired of taking care of your mother with dementia who did nothing for you all her life. How different would it be for you if you told a different story? What if you told the story of how you saw your mother with dementia as a blessing because she could no longer remember her anger and bitterness and focus it on you? What a transformed world you would live in if you created this alternate story, with these alternate emotions and thoughts. What a gift it would be for both of you at the end of her life.

Your stories can centre around people, places and things. In the example above, you could choose to keep your story going to validate not having a great relationship with your mother. Would it be true that your mother mistreated you most of your life? Yes. Would it be true that she focussed her anger and bitterness on you? Yes. But the repetition of your story would keep you in survival and wouldn't allow for the expansion of your heart into thriving that you so desire for yourself. What is also true, is that in the here and now your mother is no longer behaving that way. She no longer has the ability to do so. You now have the choice of living out the old story or letting go of the narrative by noticing your thoughts and emotions and staying in your HeartFull Response.

Remember that at the beginning, these stories helped you to make sense of your world. They helped you to move from suffering to surviving. Unfortunately you are now stuck in survival. Now, to move out of survival and along the path of this HeartFull Way is to come into an intimate awareness of all your stories.

Invitation

For this week I invite you to notice the stories you tend to tell yourself, your friends or your family. Also notice how often you tell your stories. Write them down. Your stories may begin with "I am..." or they may be a retelling over and over of past experiences. A story can be simply, "I am so tired" repeated over and over again. Once you have done this on each day of this week, I invite you to go back to your comfy place. Notice the quality of the breath that you are starting with here, and see if you can connect to that breath. Think of one of the stories you told yourself this week. Do you come out of alignment and into Picasso Response as you take notice of what stories you are replaying? If you do, simply become aware of this habit. Journey into your mind, your place of thoughts, and your belly, your place of emotions, the contributors of your once-upon-a-time stories. Notice the colours of your mind and belly flowers. Allow part of your awareness to rest here with these coloured flowers. Now allow another part of your awareness to come into your heart. What colour is this flower? Is it the same colour as your heart flower was when you found your HeartFull Response last week? If not, see if you can settle on a heart flower colour that is truly yours. Notice your three coloured flowers, one in the mind, one in the belly and one in the heart. Bring your awareness all around your mind flower and begin to allow the flower to float down into your heart. Allow your mind flower to take up residence inside your heart space and join your heart flower there. Allow your thoughts to float down into your heart, carried by your mind flower. Now do the same with your belly flower, allowing the emotions to float up to your heart. With each breath allow your heart to navigate these thoughts and emotions and guide you to your authentic wisdom. Breathe and become heartfull. Notice the colour in your heart space now. See if the colour has changed from the three different colours of your mind, belly and heart flowers, to the one colour of your HeartFull Response. Enjoy your time here for as long as it suits you. I invite you to write down the difference between the stories you experienced in your mind and belly on their own, and what you experienced as thoughts and emotions while in your HeartFull Response, with your heart helping you to navigate them. Notice whether your stories begin to shift over the week and whether the stories begin to diminish the more you allow your thoughts and emotions to centre in your heart space.

CHAPTER 5
Patterns

PATTERNS DEVELOP OUT OF YOUR LONGING TO SURVIVE. YOUR LONGING to leave suffering behind and move into the next phase, your survival. They are there to prevent suffering and avoid something that you no longer want to feel. Patterns are your attempt to move away from suffering, from pain, without having or knowing the tools to do so in a healthy way. When I see my clients' patterns I say "bravo", because I know that I am seeing a spirit that has tried and that has succeeded. A spirit that decided not be a victim and has tried to survive the best way they knew how. When you developed your patterns, you did what you had to and worked with what you knew to be available.

The patterns kept you feeling safe for a long time. The patterns are what you developed in order to avoid some kind of pain. These patterns that you created are not to be slighted. They must first be given their due. They must be celebrated and appreciated for being part of your journey to thriving. Patterns tend to develop like this: a situation comes up, you have an emotion, you have a thought, you add a story, you create a certain outcome that becomes your personal signature pattern. Then it is simply a matter of retracing your steps over and over again like a worn out path. You may have a pattern of struggle, of protection, of micro managing, of rigidity or of lack of clarity. These are a few of the paths that you may have chosen to walk over again and again without making headway on your journey. You may begin with the story or with the emotion or flip flop between the two. The outcome however, is always your same signature pattern. The way to come into relationship with your patterns is to identify your story with your thoughts and emotions and identify how they, together, led you to and into your pattern.

You might be afraid of having a close relationship, so you create a pattern of protection to keep yourself safe. To be able to create this pattern you have to tell yourself a great story over and over again about the emotion of fear or dread that comes up for you. It could be a story about others or it could be a story about yourself. An example of a story about others in this context is: "My father cheated on my mother, all men are untrustworthy and that is why I can't have a relationship. Every man that I get involved with cheats". An example of a story about yourself in this situation is: "I can't have a relationship and a career. My first love left while I was writing exams to get into law school. It never works out in the end". There are so many opportunities for stories to pop up around events in your life, and you keep telling them over and over and over. As you read in the last chapter, did these events actually happen? Yes they did. The stories came out of your deep pain, the emotions you felt and the thoughts that came up when the event took place. The stories came to make sense of the experiences for you, and the patterns came from repeating the stories over and over again. The patterns came from making these stories "matter" and then actually turning them into physical matter in your life. Now you encounter different people, places and things, but arrive at the same outcome. You take yourself right out of alignment. You live from your Picasso Response, and from the Picasso Response you are turning your patterns into living dense matter in your life and your body. The alternative is to go into your Aligned Response, move into your HeartFull Response and travel towards thriving from there.

Remember while you are playing with this that even after you are able to notice when your emotions are flaring and not aligned with your mind and your heart, even when you notice that your thoughts are telling stories and your mind is not aligned with your belly and your heart, your actual physical cells will remember the patterns that you have kept running over the years. This cellular memory, as you discovered in Chapter 1, "Surviving Through Emotions", is within the fibre that allowed you to survive almost as if on autopilot. It is within this very matter that your will to survive exists. This memory located within your cells wants to survive itself, so will try to keep running things. Instead of beginning with the sequence of emotions or thoughts first, so that you can recognize your Picasso Response and self correct, the body will trip you up. Your body will get you to trigger the pattern yourself by repeating your story to your friends or to your relations, out of your normal context. You won't even notice it is happening. It might begin with a question. For the person in the situation I described earlier in the chapter, with stories around her career and relationships, it might simply begin with a question about how she enjoyed the party she went to the previous weekend. Then without wanting to be, she is brought back into the story of not being able to have a relationship because she has no real time for work and play and it is off on the wrong path. Pattern running, emotions triggered, stories told. So before you go to this week's exercise make a pact with yourself to be gentle and cut yourself the slack needed to move through your patterns one baby step at a time. Allow yourself the space to retrace your steps one last time, and then, with loving humour, move on.

Invitation

I invite you to notice your patterns this week. Slow yourself down. Breathe. Simply make a note. You can use the space provided below. Remember, patterns were there to keep you safe so this may be a bit scary for you. Feel free to give voice to those fears as you notice the patterns. You may first wish to write down these emotions of fear. Are they apprehension, dread, panic? What emotions are coming up as you approach doing this exercise? Once you have exhausted all emotions you can then move to becoming aware of your patterns. Notice your pattern of drama, of scarcity, of confusion, of grief, of control, of discordance. Notice whatever happen to be your personal patterns of survival. Write them down. Then use this space to note your patterns as well as how you feel after the entire exercise is completed. Allow yourself to track and witness the whole process. When you feel complete with the first part of this invitation, find your cozy, comfy safe place.

Close your eyes and leave all your day behind you. Become aware of your breath. Where does it begin? Where does it end? What is its journey? Find the length of your breath. Notice your three balloons—your mind, heart and belly balloons. Check in with the colours of your balloons. See them stacked, one on top of the other. See them completely aligned. Let your breath fill them. When you inhale they expand, when you exhale they contract. You are fully in your Aligned Response. Slowly bring your mind balloon and your belly balloon into your heart. Become aware of the holy trinity within you—mind, heart and belly as one. See if your colours all merge together to form a new integrated and unified colour. Perhaps a completely different colour that now becomes your holy trinity colour and your holy trinity balloon. Breathe here and expand. You are in your HeartFull Response. Breathe here with a continuous breath—no pause at the beginning or end of your breaths. You may need to make your exhale longer than your inhale. Experiment for yourself. Take ten continuous breaths this way. Notice what you are feeling and how your heart is vibrating. Enjoy the you that is in this moment. Spend as much time here as you wish.

When you feel complete, take a couple of breaths to bring gentle movement back into your body. Let yourself slowly come back to the space that you are in. Write down how you are feeling in this moment. Notice if you can connect to a heart feeling or not. Each time you practice you will experience yourself with more intimacy. Grace yourself with this time to develop this intimacy as preparation for your HeartFull Way.

Patterns

CHAPTER 6
Your Super Powers

I HAVE COME TO DISLIKE THE PHRASE "WHAT DOESN'T KILL YOU makes you stronger". Who came up with that one? As people smile and say it to me, I smile and nod but in my head I am saying, "seriously, that's what you want to go with here?" And yet the fact that you have survived through your life means that you have developed skills that allowed you to move away from your original suffering. These skills or coping strategies created patterns with the help of your stories. As we saw in the last chapter, patterns have had you retracing your steps over and over. So you could say that these coping strategies or maladaptive skills, have formed your patterns. Hidden within each of these skills, however, is a gift. I like to refer to the gift of these skills as your super powers.

Before these skills can truly become your super powers you need to look at them in the light of where they came from. Unobserved they will be running you instead of you calling upon them at the appropriate moments to create a thriving life. These are powerful skills that helped you to survive but if you keep going to them in your day-to-day life, stuck within your old patterns, you will remain a survivor rather than a thriver. These skills have become a maladaptive coping strategy and they have been used by you while in the Picasso Response, while you were not in alignment or rooted in your heart.

Here is an example of a maladaptive skill with a hidden gift. If when you were young, you needed to watch out for what mood your parent was in as soon as you walked through the door in order to avoid conflict or violence, you might have developed a skill of hyper vigilance. This was great for you then, as a child, so you could survive. It's not so great for you now as an adult. Hyper vigilance, for example, when used on a regular basis will shift you to a constantly hyper alert mode, looking for any real or imagined danger. It will shift your thoughts, your emotions, your stories and therefore your pattern to see potential danger everywhere. It will shift your body into a fight or flight response. Therefore hyper vigilance is a maladaptive skill if used daily. The skill, if unharnessed, will take you immediately out of HeartFull Response.

If we look at what happens to you in more detail within the mind, body, spirit model, you will shift your body into its sympathetic nervous system. Your body will produce high levels of cortisol and adrenaline. It will affect your histamine levels, lowering your immune system and shutting you down from accessing your creative right brain. You will also be altering your emotions, which will change the environmental soup of your otherwise healthy DNA. Your heart generator will be impacted and your internal feelings and external vibrations will be transmitted from your Picasso Response. As you have seen by now, through the steps you have taken on your HeartFull Way, living in Picasso Response changes how you experience your life. In a state of hyper vigilance, simply walking into a room will become a stressful, unsafe experience with a potential for gathering further trauma patterns. The way you approach new people, new situations and new environments will all be painted with the same brush of alertness and wariness.

On the other hand, you will discover that this amazing hyper vigilance, if turned off when it isn't useful, and harnessed only when needed, is one of your amazing super powers. Hyper vigilance is a skill much needed by a hunter, a hiker in bad weather, a parent asked to watch over any changes in an unhealthy child, a symphony conductor, a pilot, a school yard monitor, a researcher, a trauma surgeon. There are so many applications for this super power from the ocean to the boardroom.

I see this amazing skill in my younger son when we go for deep forest walks. He notices things in the brush and is able to assess each one. He knows right away whether or not to pay one more second of attention to it or move back to enjoying the walk. This skill in him is a true super power as it comes in as needed and leaves just as easily. He is not looking for danger around every turn. His vigilance gets triggered by something real in the environment, he aligns his entire body to assess whether it is friend or foe and then moves from this beautifully aligned place. When he went skeet shooting for the first time he was able to look, watch and assess quickly and confidently, impressing all the seasoned shooters. When he went up to bat in baseball, he was able to watch all the subtle movements and changes in the pitcher to know where the ball was coming and how to best make connection.

My son's hyper vigilance is an exquisite super power when it is part of a completely aligned HeartFull Response. But he did not acquire this super power from a balanced and healthy experience. His super power was acquired as a defence against his peers who singled him out for challenges he was experiencing early in his life. He had to move through his suffering to his surviving and then into his heartfull thriving place, in order to take ownership of this super power and be able to call upon hyper vigilance rather than having it call him out. When this super power is centred in your heart and moves you towards thriving, it is both life affirming and thrilling.

To learn to harness your super powers, you need to advance on your journey. Stepping up to this part of your preparations is to ask yourself, "what did I need to do to survive? Which skills did I develop to get through those tough or traumatic experiences?" You might have to walk yourself through a few past experiences, or it might be easier for you to walk yourself through your current reactions to persons, places and things. What are the skills you needed in school? In your family life? In friendships or relationships? What are the skills you developed that you think you use very well? Once you know what these skills are you can slowly and heart-fully begin to turn them into super powers. You can begin to call upon them as needed and send them away when you are done with them. One way to joyfully turn maladaptive skills into your super powers is to come into your Aligned Response and then your HeartFull Response as many times as possible during the day. Acknowledge when a thought or an emotion comes up that is taking you out of alignment. Become aware of your process of going into Picasso Response and bringing forth a much honed skill. As soon as you notice this pattern, you will then notice what skill wants to emerge to help you through the experience. It will be there immediately, trying to help you avoid any perceived danger or discomfort and survive. Instead of using the skill right away, name it, go back to your Aligned Response, and then go into your HeartFull Response. Call upon the skill again—but now as a super power to be used in your best interest and to help you thrive. Once you feel that you have accomplished what you needed to accomplish with this super power realign once more, become even more heart-full, and you will find that your old pattern simply moved through you. You will find you are no longer stuck to the stones under your feet, but are moving forward again towards thriving.

Invitation

I invite you to notice your very own survival skills this week. See if you can trace them back to an original survival adaptation. If you can't trace them back, that is OK too. Notice how often in your day you are using your skills. You may have needed to notice what was missing in your home environment as soon as you came home so that you would know whether you were safe or not. Or you needed to see if things were neat enough to avoid intense criticism. Notice if, when you walk in your home, you notice what is wrong rather than what is right. No judgment here. Simply notice those super powers. Set aside time to write them all down and write down the context you find them in. Examine each skill and ask yourself if this skill has become a maladaptation for you in your present life. If you're not sure take a guess. Check in with how you are feeling after you finish writing. Then put everything aside and find your comfy, safe place. Spend the next few minutes noticing whether you are aligned or not, and then come into your Aligned Response. Take a few breaths here before moving on and bringing your trinity of balloons to rest in your heart space, experiencing your HeartFull Response. Think of a time that made you laugh and brought you much joy. Hold this image in your mind's eye as you spend at least five minutes breathing into your heart space, expanding and contracting your heart balloon, creating a coherent vibration in your heart. Enjoy this time with yourself.

_____

_____

_____

_____

_____

CHAPTER 7
Space, the Primary Frontier

I MUST COME FORWARD AND ADMIT I WAS AN OLD STAR TREK FAN. I loved to watch William Shatner, Leonard Nimoy and the rest of the troupe discovering new territories and having new adventures. I listened every week to "space, the final frontier". I now know that space is not the final frontier for us but rather the primary frontier. In order for you to thrive you need space—internal space and external space. All too often you are running from morning until night, overwhelming yourself by not creating external space or internal space. There is a lot of business (read busy-ness) going on in your day between yourself, your children, your family, your work, your volunteer time, your shopping etc. Sound familiar? All too often you answer too quickly, creating your own drama by not creating the internal space that you need to take that most critical moment to be present for your external world. You are in fact so overwhelmed by life that you do not have the space to take in one more thing, whether that is an invitation to play with a friend or the opportunity to entertain a new concept that could lead to some growth curve for you. There is no space to align yourself with your heart. There is no space to move into alignment with new choices and new ways of being. In order to come from an integrated HeartFull Response, you need to have heart space. The space, the time and the emptiness to connect to and with yourself.

It is in this open and empty inner space that you can create for yourselves, that you can become your own witness. To be a witness to something means that you are present to something. To be present to an experience means you offer your experience some time and space so you can become fully aware of it. To move down your path towards thriving, following your HeartFull Way, means that from moment to moment you are also becoming your own witness.

Becoming your own witness is your protection against sliding back into surviving. With the gift of space that only you can give yourself, you allow yourself to witness authentic emotions and thoughts, and realign them into your heart for integration. You give yourself the time to move into your HeartFull Response. With the gift of space, you allow yourself to be authentic and aware of your own needs, moment by moment, so that you can act in your best interest. With the gift of space you allow yourself to nurture the moments of your day with physical nourishment like food, emotional nourishment like a hug, intellectual nourishment like an idea and spiritual nourishment like connection to what you believe is divine or source energy. You become open to yourself on all levels. You move from living a full busy life to living life fully embodied in the present and engaged.

Think of your life as if it were a box. Think of your emotions and thoughts, as if they were objects you are putting into your life box. At some point that box becomes so crowded and so full that you can't possibly see inside to find anything. There is no space left in the box. There is no more room open and available for that box to take anything more inside itself. The box is closed. You close the box and place it on a shelf, never unpacking the unseen treasures hidden within. The lack of space in the box discourages you and separates you from what lies within it. So now back to your life. If you keep filling up your life with busy-ness there will be no space, no room for you to become aware of yourself in your moments. If your box is too full, you won't be able to find the pattern to untangle, the emotion to centre or the thought to understand. When you don't give yourself space, you are closed to your own self. And unlike a box you were not meant to have things stuffed inside you over and over again.

You can think of this in another way as well. Think of a kitchen counter and how amazing it feels to have a clear countertop when you are about to create a meal. Or think of a clear art table on which the negative space invites new creation. Space allows you to create something new for yourself. Space allows you to take a deep breath rather than a shallow one. Space allows you to embody your life and have room to feel what it is you are experiencing. When you can heart-fully feel your experience you can process it as an adult and decide what it is you are going to keep and what it is that you are going to discard. Space allows you to know what is real for you in the present and what is not from the present. Space allows you to become aware of what you are still holding onto from the past. Space reveals what patterns are inviting you to notice them.

Part of my work is with parents who are having some challenges with their children. I notice that many of these challenges are arising because these parents are not gifting themselves with enough space. Let me explain. In many cases, when a child comes to their parent in a moment of distress, the parents will leap into "leader" mode, to fix the situation. In this rush to move through the moment they often say something that ignites the exact opposite of the response they were hoping for. Hearing your child in distress is not easy for the most hardy of us. But taking the space to become aware that you have moved into Picasso Response, taking the space to come back through Aligned Response to HeartFull Response before you act, will give you the space that you need to be a "supportive" parent. Creating inner space allows you to witness your emotions and thoughts about a situation, and allows you to move into your HeartFull Response, so you can relate to both yourself and the other. Creating space will allow you to know what is truly here in the present moment, or what your child's distress might be triggering from your past. Giving yourself space is like giving yourself an empty canvas on which to create your next moment. Giving yourself space is giving yourself the moments in which to discover how you might nurture yourself, partner yourself or be present to yourself—and so how to be present to others. In the case of your children, space helps you discover how to support them rather than lead them so they may grow from within.

Oxytocin is known as the hug hormone, the feel-good and connected hormone. Oxytocin also mitigates the overrun of cortisol, which is a hormone that can lead to all kinds of disease including cancer. The heart makes more oxytocin than the brain. Think of that for a moment, and think of the work you have been doing with your HeartFull Response. If you can create space to embody yourself through your heart and come into your HeartFull Response more often, you are actually going to be creating more feel-good hormones. These feel-good hormones then lead to more heart-full perspectives, which then lead to more heart-full experiences, which then lead to a life of thriving and a life lived fully.

Giving yourself the time in your external space allows you the necessary moment to connect to your internal space. Connecting to internal space allows you to take up residence in, or embody, your Aligned Response and your HeartFull Response. Your heart then moves to physiologically reward you with oxytocin and a feeling and experience of heart-full thriving. The heart then learns what you chose to do and remembers your choice so that you can feel this feeling more often. What an amazing being you are! How beautifully put together. On your HeartFull Way, space is your primary frontier.

Invitation

I am going to invite you to experience space first through your breath this week. Find your safe place and then your comfy position. Be like a kitty or a puppy for a moment, wiggling into that perfect spot and perfect position. This is your opportunity to become aware and to nurture yourself. Now, find your breath. Explore the quality of your breath. Is it soft, shallow, deep, or tight? Is it fast, slow, or changing? Does it originate in your diaphragm, your throat, or your nose? Take some time to simply find the breath, its quality and its path through your body. Next, changing from your natural breath for ten breaths, breathe in and hold at the top of the breath, where your in breath ends, for two beats, and then breathe out and hold at the bottom of your breath, where the out breath ends, for two beats. Find the space at the top of the breath and the space at the bottom of the breath. See if you can float in this space between the in breath and the out breath without holding the breath. When you are finished with the ten breaths, go back to your own natural breath, and find the internal space that you created with this breathing. Perhaps your ribs will feel more open, the diaphragm looser. Allow yourself to fully feel the space. Notice the space within your body.

This week, I invite you to come back to this space between the breaths as often as you can. This internal space. I also invite you to notice the space between your activities this week— find the space between when you finish doing one thing and begin doing the next. See if you can float for a few moments in this non-doing external space between doing. See if you can acknowledge yourself between activities and actions. Fully allow yourself to embody the space inside you and all around you, by using all your senses.

A lot of feel-good feelings come with this practice of finding the space between breaths or activities. The space between doing is the still point of you. As you begin to slow down your life experiences so that you can stop and find these moments, your body may feel your moments of still point and your moments of breathing more fully. Write down what happens when you become present to these particular moments, both internal and external.

_____
_____
_____
_____
_____
_____
_____
_____
_____
_____
_____
_____
_____
_____
_____
_____
_____
_____
_____
_____
_____
_____
_____
_____
_____
_____
_____
_____

CHAPTER 8
Access Point

YOU HAVE JUST FOUND THE SPACE TO BECOME YOUR OWN WITNESS and thereby gain a more intimate relationship with yourself. Now that you have the space, you can discover your very own access point. Your access point is your point of entry on your HeartFull Way. It is the point where you will be moving from the planning and preparation stage to the actual travelling stage. On any trip or journey you can leave from various ports of call. There is no one correct access point as there is no one correct port of call. Usually your access point will be associated with a wound. You know what a physical wound is—it's a place where some part of you was cut, bruised or severed. An emotional or spiritual wound is the same. It is a place where you have been hurt or bruised emotionally or spiritually. It might be a place where connection or trust has been severed. The experience of your wound leads to a pain and the pain will ignite you to action. In the past, the action that you have been taking is an action towards avoidance—an action towards surviving, an action into your Picasso Response. You are now prepared to shift that type of action. You have created the space to become aware of your wound. You have created the space to feel your wound and then move the emotions, thoughts and patterns into your HeartFull Response. Once in your holy trinity the wound can become your motivational teacher.

The pain of your particular wound can take many forms and create many different access points. Your HeartFull Way is your journey, your personal version of access through this pain. Pain can show up as grief, or loneliness, or sadness, or depression. Each manifestation of your wound will lead you to another action which will in turn lead you to becoming aware of your very own access point in your very own way. A way you can look for your access point, is in terms of the mind, body, spirit connection, because pain distinctly manifests in those realms.

Think for a moment about your own experience or journey. How did you get this book? Was it a person or place that brought this book to your attention? Here are a few examples to illustrate how you might find your own access point, framing it through the mind, body, spirit lens. Pain in all its forms or manifestations can occur in the body the mind or the spirit.

Say you have been experiencing a lot of distress and overwhelm, in other words mind pain, from the stories that you have been telling and retelling. You go to your doctor and they suggest trying meditation or going to a yoga class. You choose the yoga class and begin to practice mindfulness during the centering, the pranayama (breathing practice) or asanas (pose practice). Through that class you begin to gain a relationship to yourself that allows your awareness to touch on your deepest survival patterns and the way you approach your life. Perhaps in a seated forward fold, you push yourself to reach your toes, going past your edge so that your muscles have no chance to lengthen slowly with each breath. Your forward fold becomes a metaphor for how you approach things in your life. Rather than being kind, slow and gentle with yourself, you become aware of how demanding, pushy and hurtful you are to yourself. You continue to push past your edge for the first few classes until you slowly become a witness to this demanding pattern. Your yoga asana has become your access point to your HeartFull Way. The distress and overwhelm of your mind was your very own pain whisperer that led you to this access point.

Another possibility is you have a skin condition—in other words a body pain—and you have spent your time making the rounds and visiting all the regular doctors and specialists. Your friend suggests a homeopathic practitioner. Through that homeopath you begin to gain clarity of your whole body and self connection and you see that your deep connection to survival has inflamed your skin condition. Your physical body was whispering to you but was not heard until it became so inflamed, so physically painful, that you had to listen. Through listening to the needs of your physical body, you were led to your access point which led you from the physical realm to the deeper layers of yourself.

And finally perhaps your child is experiencing anxiety, or psychic pain and you have not wanted to go the pharmaceutical route. Instead you have chosen to have them work with an energetic healer. Through that person you experience your child's shift after a number of energy sessions. This opens the doorway for you to realize that you have also been experiencing anxiety about your child and are now able to begin to come back to yourself. You begin to have enough ease with yourself that you can safely connect to your psychic pain and your fear patterns of survival. Your child's psychic or spiritual pain led you to this healing. The healing allowed you to discover how your sense of connection had been severed. Your first feelings of overwhelm went unheeded, so your child's spirit body wailed to you through their anxiety. This pain and their lack of connection, became your access point to this HeartFull Way.

You may experience multiple access points. They are your gifts for learning, for healing and for travelling from surviving to thriving. Remember that each access point comes from an original experience of being wounded. Allowing yourself to dip a toe into the waters of your wounding, knowing that you will not be staying there for long, will assist you in walking these sometimes painful parts of your journey. Allow yourself to briefly touch into one wound at a time. Determine if it is a wound that is being experienced through your mind, your body or your spirit. Thank your wound because it has triggered or stimulated you to find your access point. Simply become aware of this and then decide how best to walk forward through this access point. If you really have a commitment to moving into thriving, then finding these access points will assist you in finding your way through this HeartFull Way. This program is the shift you will need to blossom into thriving.

The wounds that you have experienced and the growth you experience through these various wounds to your access points, are also your gifts to share in the world. When I was young I was very close to spirit. My connection to spirit was severed at one point. I suffered under this wound and loss, and yet this very wound led me to become an energetic healer which brought me back to an even greater sense of connection. The journey that my wound invited me to take to heal it, led me to become the healer and teacher that I am today. By tracking your wounds to your access points, you can develop a greater perspective of the path you are now travelling upon. With this new perspective you can begin to reframe your wound so that you can see it as your gift. When you begin to feel that your experiences are gifts, you will step into feeling more alive, more vital and more ready to share these gifts in the world. Thriving is, after all, a celebration of your life and your relationship to life and living.

Invitation

For this week, I invite you to discover the access point that brought you here to this book and to this journey from surviving to thriving. To do that you will need to become aware of your wounds. I want you to feel safe and secure in doing this. So begin with finding your safe place. Make sure that you feel comfy and supported. Whether that support comes from a pillow, a crystal, a pet, or a painting, please set yourself up with your own personal support. Then begin to shift into your Aligned Response. Find all your pearls in alignment. Slowly bring them into your heart and find your HeartFull Response in full colour. Stay here for a few minutes. Breathe. Begin to scan the mind, the body, and the spirit that together are you. See where you might come into contact with a wound. Let your heart-fullness lead you. You don't need to linger in any of the wounds—simply make a note of them when they come up. Remember that wounds are places where you have been bruised, cut or severed. They are places that you can feel your own pain. Encountering a wound might bring you into a Picasso Response again. If it does, begin by giving thanks to your wound for being your teacher. Linger in this gratitude until you begin to feel aligned again, going back to your Aligned Response with your golden cord coming from above and reaching below.. Then move into your HeartFull Response and linger there until you are ready to see if there is another wound that is calling to you. Keep making a mental note of the wounds that come up or pause the invitation to write them down. After each exploration, return to your breath and your HeartFull Response. When you are done, and there are no more wounds that beckon your attention, linger in your holy trinity for a few minutes more. Look at the wounds that you wrote down and begin to explore them further. What aspect of you do they come from? Are they in the realm of the mind, the body, the spirit or a combination of all of them? Write down the realm you believe your wound exists in next to the name of the wound that you have written down. If you find that the wound is in the realm of the body, perhaps try and take a healing walk in nature. If it came up in the spirit realm, try using guidance cards to answer a question like "what would be best for me to focus on this week to gain gentle access through this wound?" If you find the wound exists in the realm of mind, try doing some journaling to track your thoughts for this week. Explore, play and have fun with it. See what can open up in you, to make your access points even greater.

PATH II

Noticing the Scenery

CHAPTER 9
Release

IN THE LAST FEW CHAPTERS YOU LOOKED AT EMOTIONS, THOUGHTS, stories and patterns. You looked at how they all relate to each other. You learned how to move from Picasso Response through Aligned Response, into your HeartFull Response. Before you take your next steps on your HeartFull Way, I invite you to fine tune your journey, course correcting through these next chapters. You will discover where you need to turn, or where you need to pause and take some refreshment or sustenance. To set a new course you need to release the old.

My desire is for you to truly understand that your stories and patterns are what you created to keep yourself safe and out of harm's way. Please remember that these patterns were set up by a baby, child or teenager, who did not have the skills, tools or maturity to do anything else in such challenging circumstances. Your super powers were developed to help you survive. They were the only way you knew how to adapt and therefore survive.

You are now a grown up. Your once useful adaptations have become maladaptations and are keeping you from growing into the full, self expressed, whole-hearted person that you are. They are keeping you from growing into a person capable of thriving, of keeping yourself safe and loved and fully nurtured. So you have come to the point of your journey where you are ready to release the old to make way for the new.

Release is not about denying what happened or pretending that you are something that you are not. Release is a casting forth, unburdening and making room for. Remember the example I used in Chapter 7, "Space The Primary Frontier", of the box being stuffed full of objects. There is no room to put anything new in that box unless you unburden it of some of its contents. If you want to move towards your destination of thriving, you need to make some room to maneuver. You will need to untether yourself from your current place in space. To do that you need to release the maladaptive patterns. You do this so that, rather than being tied to the past and connected to your old reactive patterns, you can begin slowly to respond to being connected to the present moment. Release creates that openness, that space to create the new possibilities that you are so craving.

At the same time, allowing yourself to release these maladaptations may bring up some of the original emotions that began your patterns. So before you move to releasing let's look at an example of how the act of release can re-ignite an original emotion—in this case fear. You might find yourself in a situation that goes something like this: you begin to release and fear pops up to stop you. The fear that pops up is fear of what is going to come next—what your journey might look like. Fear might be one of your fallback patterns like confusion or scarcity. If you are afraid you can say to yourself that you don't need to move forward, that you don't need to find that next uncharted curve on your path. But fear is only supposed to be an emotion just like any other emotion. It is supposed to be your messenger, in the moment, informing you that there is a threat to some part of you. Yet in this example, you have added your story, created your patterns and moved into Picasso Response. Now you're holding on and tethering yourself to this spot on the road. Fear of not surviving your own particular situation was what began the stories that led to the patterns. This is a moment where you do need to pause on your journey and bring yourself great understanding and compassion.

This pattern of fear may have its roots stuck deep in your past narratives. You might have been embarrassed by a teacher calling on you at school. Instead of letting the emotion you experienced be an energy-in-motion going through you, you held on to it. Instead of letting the emotion be a messenger to tell you what you needed to become aware of in yourself, and because you did not have the tools to make a different choice, you went to and held on to fear. The fear of this situation ever happening again, the need to avoid the pain of this type of situation at all costs. This led you to your story, which led you to your pattern, which led you to your super power. Your super power might be to become invisible, or to go unnoticed. That's a great super power when you're trying to get through airport security quickly. But on this part of your journey, it's not so great.

Have no fear now. You are now an adult, perfectly able to release the pattern while retaining your super power. You are an adult fully capable and ready to take on the next part of your HeartFull Way towards thriving. Release is that next step. Own your fear, name it, pick it up and hold it. Be proud of your super power and yet do not be part of it. Let the old emotion-based pattern move through you and release.

Here is an example of how you might release a pattern you could have developed with a mother who mistreated you. You don't deny that the mistreatment happened. You don't even have to forgive your mother. That step of your HeartFull Way comes later. You begin by finding something to be grateful for—then you cast forth all the rest. You release forward in time, in other words you release into the next moment from a place of being grateful. You might be wondering, in the midst of many difficult stories about your mother, what there is to be grateful for. It might seem impossible to grasp any authentically good memories. If this is the case, you can choose to be grateful for the amazing life that she gave you—the life that you are now in charge of, to grow and to make beautiful. Be grateful for the life that has allowed you to stand on the precipice of creating possibility and opportunity. Without your mother, you would have no life on this planet at this time. To be given this amazing opportunity of having a life is something that you can be authentically grateful for.

I know that you are able to find one authentic thing that allows you to express some form of gratitude in order for the old to flow into release. Your gratitude leads to your release. For some of you this might be the most difficult part. My experience with all my clients with all their various life experiences has been that there is always something that you can find to be grateful for. If you have a very deeply ingrained pattern around scarcity and have always been struggling to survive financially, you may think there is nothing available to you to be authentically grateful for. If that is the case, I invite you to think outside the box here. This is where you take real responsibility for your self as an adult and a creator—the artist within your life. Perhaps you can see the possibility of abundance in your house plant, it has so very many leaves. You can be grateful for its demonstration of "more than enough" in your life. You can thank the plant for teaching you and showing you that abundance is present and active in your life.

The shift for you is to see what it is in your life you can authentically feel grateful for, so that you can move into a state of release. The act of feeling grateful shifts you from a narrow passage to an open pathway. From this open place, you will be able to release the person, place or thing from your pattern and will be able to release any unspoken and unconscious commitments that you made with yourself within that old pattern. Your road will be made clear.

You release from your heart, from your holy trinity, releasing the past like a group of balloons released into the atmosphere, to fly up and free with room to live and connect in the moment, untethered to any agreements and patterns from the past. You release yourself to step forward into your life and embrace thriving.

Invitation

This week, I invite you to release the person place or thing involved in one of your primary patterns. Simply choose one from the last few exercises that you have done. You will be going into your HeartFull Response shortly.

It is important that you speak the words of release, so that you yourself will hear them. You will set this next piece up by saying out loud what you are grateful for and then releasing all of it. Working with the same example as above, it might go something like this. "I thank my mother for giving me this life, this blessed life. This life is mine now to live to love and to experience. I release any ties, any bonds and any commitments made within this old pattern and claim my life for my own. I release myself into this moment, free and clear." Remember, you can make up your own words, and your own ritual around release. You might want to write down what you are going to speak out loud first, speak it, and then release the paper into running water or burn it and scatter the ashes—whatever calls to you.

Before you begin your private ritual, prepare yourself by sitting in your safe space, finding your breath, going into your Aligned Response and then moving into your HeartFull Response. Remember what you learned in Chapter 3, "From Mindful to HeartFull"—that your heart is a generator of vibrations. Allow what you are grateful for come to mind. The object of that gratitude can be anything from the smile on your child's face to the tail wag of your dog. Then move into the feeling. Allow what you have chosen to be grateful for expand your heart vibrations so that the release you will experience is deep. Take time to linger in this moment of gratitude, perhaps using your continuous breathing technique, before you begin your ritual. Let your heart vibration rise until you feel ready to begin your release. Now begin your release ritual. When you are done, come back to your HeartFull Response. Enjoy the release you just experienced and openness you just created. Feel the opening up of possibilities for your HeartFull Way. Feel this release propel you forward on your journey to thriving.

_____
_____
_____
_____
_____
_____
_____
_____
_____
_____
_____
_____
_____
_____
_____
_____
_____
_____
_____
_____
_____
_____
_____
_____
_____
_____
_____
_____
_____
_____

Release

CHAPTER 10

Here Goes the Judge

IT IS TIME TO TAKE A FEW MOMENTS TO NOTICE IF YOUR INNER critic has showed up while doing the last few invitations. An essential part of this journey is to become aware of all your patterns—to notice, to look at, and to witness yourself. Can you witness yourself authentically, or do you begin to get off focus by distracting yourself and passing the emotional hot potato with stories about your stories. I have had clients who are making amazing progress until they take a fork in the road of their journey with stories about how they now see that they wasted the last five years of their life. Rather than becoming aware of their progress, witnessing their moments of success and feeling differently inside themselves, they go back to their patterned emotions because the pattern is still the most comfortable place to be. They pass the emotional hot potato. Rather than the witness, they occupy another seat in the courtroom. They judge themselves. They disrespect the perfection of the tools they used to survive, and discredit their own particular art of survival. I must say here that I know that surviving is not the end goal of my clients, or of anyone reading this book, but it is what you, in all your intelligence, have been able to do so far. Now you are here and aware and present enough to your experiences to be looking towards something deeper and greater. There has been nothing wasted in any of your experiences.

Notice if you have been judging yourself. Notice if you have a feeling of being "less than". This is a judgment—and judgment is not an emotion. Judgement is an action of thought. It is an interpretation, an evaluation and a diagnosis. As an interpretation it physically activates your body, telling it to keep on high alert. It sends a message to keep your body in fight, flight or freeze mode needing to know what you need to pay attention to next. The need to judge comes out of a need to survive, and it cuts off your access to your heart and your HeartFull Response. It comes from a place of feeling like you have no other options but to judge and evaluate if you are going to be safe. It sinks you deeper into survival and into your Picasso Response. It can be one of the last patterns that your body wants to release.

Your mind believes that judging kept you safe and alive. Your belly believes that you could avoid discomfort if you could only judge the situation in your favour. Your heart is left in no-man's land. You may not feel safe if you decide to stop judging. This belief, that judgment keeps you safe, is deeply rooted in your Picasso Response, and is going to kick, scream and try to convince you that there is no way that you can survive without it. This belief is going to try to keep bringing you back to judgment again and again. If you know this is going to happen, you will be prepared, and you will give the judging part of you something else to do—transforming it into a super power. Because in some ways that voice is correct. You needed judgment to survive. But what is also true is that you no longer want to survive you want to thrive. So you can say, "thank you but no thank you" to this inner judge. You can finally say no to your inner critic because to continually judge yourself is to inflict violence on yourself. Think of how often you have looked at yourself in the mirror, judged yourself and said unkind words to yourself. This kind of constant judgment is a violent act against self. So yes, you did survive using judgment and now you can release it. Your judgment was an act against self. You are now ready to place it amongst your wonderful super powers in your tool box to use when appropriate to assist you.

Judgment does not come to the party alone. Judgment usually comes in a triad with control and perfectionism. To be able to be in control of your circumstances you judge your situation, you judge others, and you judge yourself in relation to the situation and to the others. When you make these judgments, you set yourself apart from the person place or thing and make yourself superior to, or less than what is at the centre.

If you have decided that you are less than in a situation, you will then decide how best to control that. Perhaps you will choose not to attend a party. If you have decided that you are superior to the situation, you will then decide how to control the situation to keep it the same. You might choose to sit in a particular seat at a restaurant to keep your eye on the kitchen. Either way this control and judgment will lead you to seek perfectionism, where you try to ensure your survival by never making mistakes. It can be a challenging survival cycle to be in and a very difficult one to move out of. This triad of survival skills becomes completely unconscious. You don't even notice that you are repeatedly judging your place as above or below others, or judging your environment as meeting your standards or not. This is how you survived at home, in school, at camp, or in group activities. Now at this part of your HeartFull Way, you will have to choose to become aware, present and open to noticing when and how often this trio shows up for you. You stay present and allow yourself to create the space for witnessing with ease. And to above all not judge yourself when you see this triad show up and so keep yourself tethered to your spot on the road.

You are not born looking for any of these traits. You are not born a judge, or a controlling person or a perfectionist. You are born experiencing the moment. Each moment is teaching you through your experiences. Then you choose in the moment what you are going to do about what you experience—based on whether the experience is life affirming and safe or threatening to you in some way? In your world to have developed these super powers you must have had experiences where you felt threatened in some way. This is where you practice much self-compassion around your patterns, and you practice release. You may want to look over the last chapter again in the context of your relationship to this triad.

Control comes from your external world. You bump up against a situation that makes you feel uncomfortable or that stimulates or triggers you. In this very moment you can choose to leave your connections to your Aligned Response and move into a Picasso Response or you can stay connected and move into your HeartFull Response. From your Picasso Response, you can protect yourself and experience the same thing in the same way again by choosing judgment, control and perfectionism or you can open yourself to a completely new possibility by bringing yourself back into your holy trinity. Here is the fork in your journey.

Staying with judgment is what you know as familiar, but you already know the next step leads you to control and then to trying to make yourself or the situation perfect. It is exhausting and life sucking and does not lead to thriving. I have clients who follow this path and rather than allowing themselves those extra fifteen minutes to sleep in, they are judging, controlling and perfecting their homes almost before their feet get to touch the ground. If one nail has a slight chip, they are on high alert. If their children don't step in line that day, they are full of stress. They see their children as something they need to fix, change and perfect. To do this is to react rather than respond or create anew. Trying to get it right is an act of striving or grasping not a state of thriving. Trying to get it perfect is not thriving. Controlling rather than allowing the space for your journey and for your families journey, is not thriving. To turn on yourself and your family in this way is to bind yourself to survival. It is to bind yourself to pain. There is nothing perfect in this life and world, and yet it is all perfect. In a garden, each leaf and flower adds to the whole beauty you perceive. You don't look at a tulip in your garden and judge whether its stalk is the same as the one next to it or it has identical leaves to the others or that all the reds match perfectly or control the heights to match each other. Why would you ever do any of this to yourself?

If you leave the realm of the internal, your HeartFull Response, and focus on the realm of your external environment, you will be brought backwards into your Picasso Response. If you seek to avoid and end the pain and discomfort of your situation, you could miss the message of your emotions—your energy-in-motion. When you miss your internal cues, your Picasso Response can lead you to judge, then control and then try to perfect yourself or the person or situation in front of you. Are you going to repeat the same experiences out of old patterns that you no longer need, or are you ready to release your inner judge, your inner controller and your inner perfectionist and move towards healing and thriving? At this juncture in your HeartFull Way they can no longer help you navigate the terrain. It will take courage as you manoeuvre forwards, but you already possess courage, as you are here.

Invitation

I invite you to take a few moments to name your inner judge, perfectionist, and controller. See them as three separate beings. Have fun with this and give them names. I named my perfectionist Ms. P. Naming them will help you see them as parts of you that you can speak with. Begin by having a bit of a get-to-know-you conversation. Once you feel comfortable with that, you can tell your inner perfectionist that each time it shows up in your life this week you have decided that it will have something new to do in your life. You are going to give it a task—something completely different from what it is used to doing. Your inner perfectionist might like focusing on tidying up an area of your desk and making it perfect. It might like to get a colouring book and colour within the lines. Be creative here and give your judge, your controller and your perfectionist something to occupy themselves with other than your usual pattern. Create something to keep them busy and out of your way for this week. Enjoy your time with them as they get busy with their new jobs. Write down your experience with each one and which tasks seemed to work best for you. Play and enjoy giving constructive expression to these different parts of yourself. Once you have them instead of them having you, you may begin to call upon them as your super powers. If they ever get out of hand, you can go back to this invitation as often as you like. Also take time this week to practice your continuous breathing and both your Aligned Response and HeatFull Response.

CHAPTER 11

It Isn't Personal

YOUR LIFE ISN'T PERSONAL. THAT IS A DIFFICULT CONCEPT FOR MOST people to hear, but an important one for thriving. If you are in survival, chances are that your childhood became very personal to you. There was some event that you personalized and began to suffer from. At some point you no longer wanted to suffer so you began to develop your patterns to help you move from suffering to surviving. We have tracked this part of your journey in the previous chapters. The bridge that helped you to move from suffering to surviving, your patterns, developed your super powers. Now we will take a few steps backwards to allow you to sprint forwards.

If you have experienced trauma or dysfunction of the family system, or trauma or pain in your health, and if that state of suffering in pain, is still lingering, you have definitely personalized your life experiences. Even if you do not label the past as traumatic but rather speak of it to your friends in terms of "down home craziness and insanity", you have personalized your life. If what your parents said and the rationales they gave you for the behaviour you experienced seemed completely out of touch with your reality and your version of common sense, there will be trust and safety issues to deal with. And if these trust and safety issues are still part of your personal life story, your state of suffering will still be lingering just below the surface of your survival. Suffering's lingering closeness will act as a magnet, keeping you attached to survival and making your sprint towards the next leg of your journey difficult.

I would like to underline here that you have certainly experienced traumas. To survive is to steel yourself against an event, a situation, or a person. It is embedded in the very nature of surviving. You are surviving something. And if you are continuing in survival mode long after the moment of trauma, you have personalized the person place or thing that traumatized you. On your HeartFull Way moving to thriving is to notice your bridges—your patterns—and move across them.

When you were a child your survival and safety were dependent on those adults who were taking care of you. Your sense of safety and security came from your perspective of seeing your parents capable, in charge and taking care of things. When your survival and safety were threatened by the behaviour of the adults in your life, when, from your perspective, they were not living up to what you required to feel at ease and whole, you needed to make sense of your world and make it as alright as possible. You needed to create a sense of safety for yourself in order to keep functioning.

As a child you used your imaginal mind to survive. Instead of seeing the adults as crazy, or not capable of parenting, you saw them as the sane ones, and the capable ones and you personalized the things that were happening as things that have to do with you instead of with them, and you suffered.

Here is an example of personalizing from a child's imaginal brain. Say you are 4 years old. Your father always told you to brush your teeth but you thought it was too much of a bother. Your father suddenly dies and you say to yourself from this imaginal mind, "Dad would not have died if I had only brushed my teeth." You suffer under this notion, and in order to survive that suffering you tell yourself another story. You create other emotions and all this finally develops into your patterns.

Suffering comes before surviving. Some people stay in the suffering phase forever, some for a few years. At some point you decided, consciously or unconsciously, to move through your suffering into surviving. You are now deeply in survival mode and cannot yet bridge the stage of surviving to thriving. Step by step, through your HeartFull Way you will acquire all the tools you will need to build your bridges to thriving, just as you built your bridges to surviving.

When you begin to bring awareness to the way personalizing oper-
ates in your life, you begin to build this bridge. With awareness you
begin to disentangle yourself from the personal.

Within each of you is an inner child who, when triggered or stimulated, behaves the same as the child who first experienced the traumatic
event. The child who experienced the adults acting in such a confusing
way that it left your need for safety and security constantly unmet. The
child who suffered with feelings of fear and dread. This means that you
are still expecting the adults around you to behave in a certain sane
way, and it means that when they don't, you personalize the situation
and think it is about you. The adults however, are now your peers. They
are not responsible for what happened to you in your past and they are
not responsible for securing your present. Yet you are still acting out
from your child's place of fear and dread—and suffering.

Here is an example of how you could be making things personal as
an adult. It's an example from my own life and it's the last time I made
my life personal. I had an appointment with the hairdresser—my first
one after one of my surgeries. It had been a pretty miserable recov-
ery and I was looking forward to getting pampered. In fact, the week
before I had popped a stitch and needed to cancel my hair appointment in order to go to the doctor's office. So you get the picture. I was
both in a vulnerable state and very excited. My emotions were running
the show and they were way out to the left. I was already in a Picasso
Response, which made me even more vulnerable to the magnet of past
sufferings. I arrived at the salon expecting to be called in any minute.
In Picasso Response you do experience these expectations. My hairdresser came out and called another woman in. She then came back
out and sat next to me to apologize: she had double booked the slot
by accident and she wondered if I could come back the next day. Well,
acting as the polite obedient child, I said yes. I went to my car and my
mind began to run its stories because I was triggered and needed to
make it about me. I cried and wondered why I wasn't chosen, what
was wrong with me, why the other client was favoured. I had just gone
through all this surgery—why didn't I deserve the haircut? Again you
get the picture. There were a whole lot of "I"s. My emotions went left
and my thoughts went right and there was no Aligned Response or
any way to get to HeartFull Response. I had completely personalized
an event that had nothing to do with me and everything to do with a
computer glitch, or a booking mistake. My mind, body and spirit were

completely out of alignment. I was back to actual suffering. I had to become aware again of emotions, of stories and of patterns. I had to create the space to find my Aligned Response and build the bridge to my HeartFull Response. Only from that place could I recognize that the event wasn't personal and get back to thriving. The old pattern was very entrenched and it took me a whole day to do this.

After that I never let it happen again. I realized then and there that it was never worth personalizing my life and losing a whole beautiful day climbing through something that had nothing to do with me. Your life is not personal. The lack of the personal is freeing. The absence of the personal in life allows you to release the state of underlying suffering that has been lingering. It allows you to keep sprinting towards thriving. Enjoy the feeling of the air on your skin as you now move more quickly on this leg of your journey.

Invitation

This week I invite you to notice the times when you are personalizing events in your life. It doesn't have to be dramatic. It could be something like saying someone cut you off while driving. I really like this one as an example. I hear it all the time. "He cut me off!" But chances are he didn't even see you. He was going about his business, driving to his next appointment. He had no thoughts about you. He was immersed in his own need to get somewhere. Was the result that you got cut off from your driving plan? Yes it was, but the driver did not set out to do this to you. It was not personal at all. Yet you interpreted the situation in a personal way. Simply make a note of when these situations arise this week. Note what you were feeling just before these moments happen. Note what you feel when you personalize the event. Were you in your Picasso Response or Aligned Response? Were you present in your body? Or were you telling stories and letting your emotions run? Become the witness and observe. What might have happened that has nothing to do with you? Make the correction in your body by writing down the observation or truth of the situation. If you wrote about the example from above with another driver on the road, you would write down your personal story of being cut off, and the emotions and thoughts that were running through you at the time. Then you would write down the observation free of the personal, something like: the person in the grey car was driving, moving to their next commitment of the day. Now write down how you feel in the presence of the event, free of the personal. Did something open up for you and give you space? Finally, spend a few minutes in your HeartFull Response to feel the safety and security that comes from releasing the personal. Feel what exists in this place of freedom from the personal. Let the feeling spread from your heart throughout your whole body. Let all of you re-

learn this place of freedom—this place that existed before you began to personalize. Feel it in your entire being.

CHAPTER 12
From Confusion to Clarity

CONFUSION IS A VERY COMMON PATTERN THAT A LOT OF PEOPLE GET into early in life. You might find your teen using it just as much as you are. Confusion can begin as a way of avoiding something in your early years—something that you didn't have the tools to cope with or to process. Something that made you feel insecure, afraid and unsafe. Something that to you was best always avoided. Confusion became your go to pattern. It might have been a neighbour asking how things were going at home. If that was a question you never wanted to answer, you would act confused to deflect anymore personal questions. Confusion might have been in response to your first heartbreak. Perhaps it showed up when you were feeling conflicted about choices you wanted to make for yourself, but felt compelled to toe the line and do as you were told. There are many reasons that someone might go to confusion as a maladaptive tool. You are in good company if you can relate to confusion being one of your tools. If you find the answer to many of the questions that you ask yourself is "I don't know", confusion has become part of your repertoire. Why do I feel this way? "I don't know." What is my body saying yes to? "I don't know." What do I feel I need to be my best self? "I don't know." What is blocking me? "I don't know." The questions are endless, but the answer is always "I don't know".

The more you repeat your stories, thoughts, emotions and patterns the more you are left with "I don't know". Confusion sets in when there are no in-the-moment, present, authentic responses and input. In other words, confusion is the habit when your habit is to live in your past or future, live from your stories or your emotions linked to thoughts. Confusion can also arise when you let your emotions dictate your choices or when you let your thoughts run the show. You become confused when you are looking ahead on your path or behind from whence you came and you are not noticing the scenery right where you are. When you are in your Picasso Response, there is no place for in-the-moment access to your present authentic processing. Confusion gives you a reason to take yourself out of your HeartFull Response. However, as you have learned, it is in the present moment, in your HeartFull Response, that your patterns disappear. It is in the present moment that confusion can melt away and you can become authentically available to yourself. This is the moment for you to connect inward and become your own witness. This is the moment to become aware of what is actually happening and what you are actually feeling—when your thoughts, emotions and heart are working together.

By becoming aware of your own confusion you get to see how it actually kept you protected at some point. There has been a huge upside for you within your confusion. Your job right now is to find what that upside is. If this feels challenging for you and you find another "I don't know" cropping up, flip the question on its head. What would be the downside of getting crystal clear for yourself? What would you be risking or losing if you stopped being confused?

Let's explore these questions through an example. Perhaps you have been hanging out in the muddy waters of confusion so you'll get to hang out in a relationship that no longer works for you. One possible upside of staying in this relationship rather than leaving it is that you can retain the status quo. If you stay confused and stay put, you might not have to go to work and worry about making money, you won't have to move or start a new life, you can avoid taking responsibility for your part in the relationship going south, or your kids get to stay with the same friends, family and schools. There might be a lot of upsides in the confusion of "I don't know". These are only a few of the possibilities.

When you think of confusion, in terms of your children, when they are saying no to you, they are actually saying yes to themselves. When a child says "no I don't want to set the table", somewhere inside their body, they are saying yes to something else. It might be "Yes I want to finish reading this post my friend sent out." This is the teaching moment. If you choose to enter into a power struggle at that moment, confusion will be set up as a pattern for both of you. They will never be able to access what they are feeling, what their body is saying yes to. Remember the earlier question of "What is my body saying yes to?" If you answered "I don't know", this might have been where your pattern for confusion began. If you and your child both move into Picasso Response at this point, your pattern will continue and your child's pattern will begin. Neither one of you is authentically present,

So what if you got clear? Well, you would have to take a lot of responsibility, do a lot of growing and finally move from surviving your circumstances to thriving into your life. That is both big and glorious. The more you can stay in your holy trinity and present to yourself, the greater your capacity for life, living and thriving. And yes, that can feel very different for you at first.

If your life has been filled with drama caused by your confusion, rather than the ease that comes with clarity, look at the fuzziness that you might be holding on to. Your personal drama could look like a horror story, an action adventure, a medical mystery, or a legal drama. To become clear and focussed, to release confusion, means to become a witness to this survival pattern. When you release the drama by becoming your very own audience or witness to it, you allow your present moment emotions to come in. These emotions are there to let you know that you are in fact doing something differently. As you have discovered already they are your messengers. If you allow your emotions to deliver the message and leave your body (remember the ninety second rule), they can be a potent ally. They can confirm the courageous step that you are taking by letting go of confusion. Your thoughts also speak to you in these moments of clarity. They might be saying, "Whoa, you're actually doing this. Good for you". Now allow those thoughts and emotions to leave by saying a few positive things about your choice like, "I am brave and courageous. I am going to take this slowly and be kind to myself. I am going to choose clarity over confusion". Hearing yourself, and being able to really see and acknowledge yourself with these statements, allows thoughts and emotions to move, and brings you back into your Aligned Response so that you can then bring yourself back to your HeartFull Response. At this stage of your HeartFull Way, the process of witnessing, realignment and release may take some time. But if you practice being in the moment authentically and fully this process takes minutes.

Being unfocussed and unclear may be your way of avoiding standing out, of being found unworthy, or of being hurt—pain that mostly stems from making your life personal. Allowing these emotions and thoughts to run you by staying in confusion will keep you forever in survival mode as these will trigger your constant fight, flight, freeze response. But if you allow the moment to be your ally, it will alert you, as we discussed in the last chapter, to profound realizations about the things you are making personal. Knowing that you have gone to the personal will allow you to move gracefully and come into the holy trinity of your HeartFull Response, so that you can process these emotions and thoughts, and come to know what is authentic for you in this moment. You can then respond quickly, not in the past or future, but in the here and heart-full now. Your deep power lies in the ability to get clear for yourself. Getting clear will enable you to know what you need to release, know what you need to forgive and ultimately know where you really need to love, for your life, for your living and for your thriving.

Invitation

For this week I invite you to notice where you are unclear, unfocussed or fuzzy. Notice when you answer yourself with "I don't know". Ask yourself very specific questions to get started, like "what is my body saying yes to right now?" What are you thinking? What are you feeling? What do you need to be your best self? What is blocking you? Write down both the questions you asked yourself and then the fuzzy or confused answers that you came up with. Take the time to explore what the upside has been to hanging on to your confusion and what the downside of gaining clarity has been for you. At any time you begin to feel overwhelmed or blocked go to your safe and comfy place and find your Aligned Response. Then take ten breaths and move into your HeartFull Response: visualize the triad of your flowers resting safely and securely there. Bring your attention to your tailbone and send out a hollow cord that ends in the centre of the earth. This is your grounding cord. As you inhale imagine gathering up all your confusion, and as you exhale send this confusion down the grounding cord and out of your body. Do this five to ten times. When you've become authentically present to yourself in this moment, go back and see if the answers now flow for you. Over this week, see if you can choose one situation to get clear on. Practice this clarity daily and notice how it makes you feel. Write down your gentle observations of yourself. Remember to go back to your HeartFull Response at any time that you feel unsafe or unkind with yourself. You are moving the pebbles away that hamper you on your journey. You are making your way through this life-affirming pilgrimage.

CHAPTER 13

The Lights Are on but Nobody's Home

HAVE YOU EVER BEEN DRIVING SOMEWHERE WHEN, BEFORE YOU realize it, you have arrived at your destination only to wonder how you actually got there? You have a feeling of waking up when you arrive, without having been present to your journey of getting there. Your mind was off somewhere and your body was on automatic. The lights were on but nobody was home. This oh so familiar process is sometimes called dissociation and it can be a jarring experience when you suddenly land back in your body and realize that you were off somewhere else during a critical time. This example of dissociation while driving a moving vehicle happens more often than is safe or healthy for people—and it does illustrate that your body can work and go on in a dissociative state albeit an unsafe one.

Mostly you will dissociate when you are overwhelmed by your thoughts. Dissociation will cause you to be in an unsafe state, as you are not in your Aligned Response, and present to yourself and your situation. In this state you are unable to make thriving choices for yourself. The thoughts that are primarily overwhelming you in these circumstances do not even exist in your present. They are not coming from what you are seeing around you on your path or in this example, on the road. When you are dissociated, you are not thinking, "there is a white car in front of me", or "there is the stop sign". If you were thinking these thoughts, you would be present to the moment. The thoughts you are engaging in are coming from either your past or your future. You might be thinking of what happened in the morning with your kids, or all the things that you still need to get done in your day. These thoughts are not coming from the present you, that is simply driving from point A to point B. It is truly amazing when you can notice this type of dissociation happening, and explore how your body works and is able to do this.

This dissociative pattern is how you chose to survive when your body suffered with any type of trauma that overwhelmed you. The emotion of being overwhelmed was your response to your suffering, and dissociation was your survival response to feeling overwhelmed. You might have been overwhelmed by the pain of separation—by physical, spiritual or emotional suffering, or by the intensity of an insane environment. Within the human experience, the possibilities for trauma and pain are endless. The situation you experienced became your suffering. Notice your own pain—perhaps it bubbles up as this information lands for you. Take it in for a moment. Notice what happens when you take a breath and give yourself a moment of acknowledgment. Notice how powerful it is to stop denying yourself and instead acknowledge your own experience. The thought or recognition of your suffering may bring up emotions and you may experience tears or anger. Notice the experience of your suffering and your body's desire to survive the thoughts and emotions you are having. Your body is deciding to survive yet again, and this may lead you to try to dissociate—even now as you continue to read this and as you continue to try and stay present to your choice of reading this chapter.

As parents, you may experience this dissociation as fixation. When you get triggered by your child and you can't bear to look at yourself, you fixate on something completely different. This act of dissociation might transfer from one experience with one child to another experience with your other child. Let me explain how this might work. You begin a discussion with child number one about their behaviour and the following occurs. You think you are all prepared and everything is going to go as you expect it to. That's problem one, as expectations are probably one of the top causes of your pain. The conversation goes sideways and what your child says about you becomes a trigger or stimulus for a past experience. You compound your suffering by taking everything that she has said personally. You are now fully in your Picasso Response. Instead of taking the time to come into your Aligned Response, then move into your HeartFull Response, in order to get in touch with what you feel and need in the moment, you are overwhelmed by the moment and you choose to dissociate. To keep your self in this dissociated state, you must fixate on something else. So you march down the hall and see that child number two's room is a mess. You now fixate on the state of his room, creating another incident, and the result is that you never have to deal with the first trigger and the ensuing emotions that you experienced. You have dissociated and fixated as a way to stay out of being authentically present to yourself. Because you have chosen to dissociate from yourself you have also dissociated from your children. You are not available to be "present and accounted for" with them. You are not able to hear their feelings and needs.

The absolute discomfort of the moment will sometimes override any of the well learned tools you have so far garnered, to stay present to yourself. The only option you can see for yourself in the moment is to dissociate. Probably, later at night when you are alone with yourself, you can begin to dip your toe back into the experience. You see that you didn't acknowledge yourself and you didn't acknowledge your own means to survive. Allow the authentic experience to come into focus, come into the holy trinity of your HeartFull Response, all your pearls in your heart, and authentically allow the trauma to be real for you. Then slowly begin the process of releasing the now habitual movement toward dissociation. Step forward toward thriving with gentle, delicate baby steps. This is your life affirming journey. This is not an easy time but it is an exquisitely intimate time that you will share with yourself—one you will come to honour deeply within yourself. If you need to at this point, go back to Chapter 9, "Release", until this process becomes second nature. This is your opportunity to repair and heal.

My invitation to you is to see that dissociation is one of your super powers. It kept you alive and surviving in the past when you were too young, too little and too vulnerable to survive any other way. But my promise to you is to guide you to thriving and this automatic dissociation takes you out of your present embodied heart self that you have been cultivating through the previous chapters. It takes you into thought emotions rather than the experience of embodied heart feelings in the now.

❀

Think back to earlier in this chapter when you explored dissociation in the context of a parent dissociating from a trigger related to one
child by fixating on an issue with another child. You may have spent
a moment relating to the pain of this situation and acknowledging
one of your own traumatic experiences. What's interesting to notice
is what happened next: you pick up the book again and as you begin
to read you seem "under control" once more. Now if I had asked you
how you are feeling at that moment, you would have probably told me
the story about what happened—thoughts and emotions entwined.
You would dissociate by taking yourself into your immediate past, and
would not answer how you are feeling in the actual present. So to
clarify the conversation might go something like this: I ask you "how
are you feeling?" and you answer me by describing the situation with,
"I was remembering what happened to me when...". instead of taking
a beat to go into your heart. In your HeartFull Response you might
say "I am feeling bereaved". However, in your Picasso Response you
would be more likely to say "I am feeling betrayed". What is the difference between these two responses?

"I feel betrayed" is a thought emotion. Why is this a thought
emotion and not an authentic feeling? You are trying to think your
emotions. The word "betrayed" is an evaluation of a situation. It is not
an emotion. So it is a thought emotion, describing what you think happened to you. The betrayal, which was part of your story and perhaps
even a pattern of yours, happened in the past. Feelings only exist in
the present. If you stayed in your present body within your holy trinity,
the feeling you might have would not be "betrayed", because you are
not presently being betrayed. It is not happening now. However the
feeling might be bereaved, as you realize that not only might you have
been betrayed in the past but you also betrayed yourself by dissociating from your heart and your nature as a pattern that you continue
to practice.

So notice this pattern of dissociation and be OK with it. Your pain
may seem too big right now as you first look upon it. It may be like
a deep dark pothole that you will trip into and never get out of. The
dissociation super power, gives you the grip you need to pull yourself
out of the pothole should you fall in. You can't release dissociation as a
pattern, without replacing it with your grounding HeartFull Response,
where you can be present for yourself.

Another way you could dissociate to your thought emotions besides fixation is through a spiritual practice. If you're dissociating through a spiritual practice, you're abandoning yourself and your own feelings to connect to something greater than you. You believe that you have replaced your dissociative pattern with a healthy spiritual practice only to find that you have discovered yet another and perhaps more socially accepted way to dissociate. This is not to say that a spiritual practice is not a sacred part of being human. It absolutely is, if it is a grounded and embodied practice and not a place to hide from self. Often, however, what I see are individuals who can't bear the pain of their human experience, so they go dissociate off into a spiritual practice. They leave their bodies to play in this other realm as an alternative dissociative state. They abdicate any personal choices and responsibility. They abandon their bodies, and lose touch with their emotional messengers. When they describe their week with all their challenging stories based in patterns and I ask what they are feeling, they usually say "joy". This is a grave disconnect or dissociation. These clients of mine will usually be experiencing physical pain because it is the only way that the body has left to get its messages through. You may have heard of the saying, " what you resist persists". These clients are resisting or dissociating from their bodies. They are not taking responsibility for their behaviour by facing what the moment is delivering to them, one emotion, thought or pattern at a time.

This is not to ever minimize your fully embodied and ever important connection to self and source. It is also not to say that you are not an infinite being with connections to all kinds of other realms and guides. It is however an invitation to notice where and how your own personal super powered dissociation happens, whether in the physical or non physical form. Notice whether you tend to go into the physical realm of fixation, or to the non physical realm of your spiritual practice. When you recognize what your go-to place is, you can take your next steps toward thriving. You can move into your own HeartFull Response and experience your authentic relationship to yourself. You can now have all your lights on and be very present in your home.

Invitation

I would like to invite you to notice the arc of your dissociation this week. If nothing is triggering you I invite you to make a call or have a visit with someone that might trigger you in a relatively small way so that you can work with this energy. Remember—I said in a small way. You are only going to dip your toe in this practice for now. When you get triggered, notice how long you allow yourself to stay in the emotion of your pain before you head to distracting thoughts, to fixations or to a spiritual lift-off and a running away or dissociation that takes you away from your experience. This is the just one of the steps that you will take on the path of being present, as the next few chapters will begin to move you out of your past and into your present more and more, so that you can create your thriving future. It will be very important this week to write down any-thing that has come up for you around your triggers to dissocia-tion, and then to end by coming into your safe and comfy place. Support yourself with pillows and props Take a few natural breaths. Find your three pearls— one in your mind, one in your heart and one in your belly. Imaging a golden cord coming from the sky through the centre of your head and threading through all three pearls. Allow this golden cord to go through your belly pearl and continue down to the centre of the earth with a large weight on its end. This is your Aligned Response. Allow your belly pearl to slide up the cord to your heart, and your mind pearl to slide down the cord to your heart. This is your holy trinity of pearls. This is your HeartFull Response. Breathe into your heart space and breathe into your holy trinity for at least five to ten breaths. Focus in on your heartFull Response. When you feel complete come back to your own natural breath for a couple more breaths and bring gentle movement to your head, your hands, your feet and your eyes.

🐞

CHAPTER 14

Distress or Stress?

MOST OF YOU PROBABLY EXPERIENCE YOUR STRESS AS DIS-STRESS OR the more commonly seen word distress. You probably find yourself in distress on a daily basis. You might feel like you are at the edge of your limits and, that one more thing puts you into a state of overwhelm and distress. I believe the place to start when learning about dis-stress is with a brief discussion on what your edge is or means and what stress is. If you have taken yoga before you will have heard a teacher talking about your edge—the concept of the edge. If you have been overwhelmed by traumatic experiences you might have dissociated from your body, as we discussed in the previous chapter, and lost access to your ability to be in touch with your edge. I see this all the time in classes. Some students race into a pose very deeply, passing through their edge and therefore not being in touch with that beautiful moment of pulling back and away from stressing the body like an overused elastic. As you know, if you quickly stretch an elastic it lengthens and goes back to its original size. But if you slowly apply pressure to the elastic its entire size will lengthen and stay long. It is the same with your muscles and the same with your life. Going past your edge in a stressful situation does not serve you or grow your capacity for thriving. It produces a yoyo effect that affects your mind, body and spirit health and well-being.

Stress on the body is a natural phenomena. It is actually a healthy and functional part of our physiology. When you apply stress to a bone, that bone actually gets healthier and creates more density. When you apply stress to a muscle, you have the opportunity to build that muscle and make it stronger. When you bring stress to an activity it produces a clear and more narrowing focus which can allow you to succeed at a specific task. So stress is part of a life lived fully. Stress is a messenger. It tells you how much pressure you need to exert in a physical or mental task. It tells you when that amount is too much to be a helping hand. This feedback loop is only possible if you retain your intimate connection to your heart and your holy trinity.

Stress becomes dis-stress when you bring the stress into either the realm of the emotional body or the mental body. In other words, you transform stress into distress when you begin to tell stories and allow your emotions to hang on past the ninety second rule. Usually when you say you feel stressed or someone is stressing you out, you are experiencing an emotion and you are telling yourself a story about the pressure being applied. You are allowing yourself to come out of an Aligned Response and go back into your Picasso Response. You have allowed yourself to be triggered by your experience and you have gone back to one of your old patterns. It might be that you are overwhelmed or experiencing frustration and you are telling yourself a story about how you think you don't have enough time for something. Take a minute and think about the last time you felt stressed. See if you can isolate what emotion and story you were experiencing. I think that you will be able to see that your stress was not a healthy call to action for your body. It didn't help your body to muster its energy and focus, but rather it resulted in an emotional and mental experience of distress.

To be able to move out of distress is to be able to tease out the various parts of your experience. In the situation above, if you had noticed the emotion—your energy-in-motion—telling you that something was not working for you and moved further into you HeartFull Response, you would have been able to listen to yourself and move away from what was not working for you. Or if you started with the story of not having enough time for anything, and moved that into your heart, you would have been able to gain the understanding and wisdom of the situation to move on. Instead of doing either of those things, perhaps you turned to your child who wanted to speak to you and said that he was stressing you out.

There is another choice. When you are in your HeartFull Response, you can turn to him and say, "I am feeling ... in the presence of the moment." You can insert your own feelings—angry, rushed, vulnerable. Once you are able to stop yourself from going into your Picasso Response, able to become aware of your emotions and the stories you are telling yourself, you can go back and check on the message you are actually receiving. You can become curious and see if they are your programmed emotions, thoughts and stories from your past—in other words your pattern—or a present emotional messenger asking you to pay attention. You can begin to evaluate if the emotions you are experiencing are authentic and in-the-moment, a healthy messenger for you or if they are your conditioned fight or flight reflexes getting activated again.

What are conditioned fight or flight responses? Without spending the rest of the book going through the science, I will describe your natural response to a perceived danger. When an emotion, thought or sense comes up for you that tells you something is not working in your environment, the body has a number of choices. If you did not experience childhood traumas or dysfunctions, your heart rate might speed up, a little adrenalin may flow, cortisol levels may rise, and your body might increase its histamine output, but not too much of a response will kick in. You won't have suffered or moved into survival mode and you won't now go on alert to any threats to your survival.

However, if you have suffered early traumas, you will be looking out for these threatening experiences. This is where you have honed your super powers. So in the present, if you sense something is not working and before you can get into your HeartFull Response, your body takes over. You now move from the healthy edge of stress to the programmed unhealthy patterns of distress. You move from a parasympathetic response or relaxed response to a sympathetic response or alert response. Two completely different nervous systems of your body. Your body now has a few choices within the sympathetic response. It can go to flight, which might take you to running away from your emotions with dissociation or fixation perhaps to a TV show. It can go to fight, which might take you into an argument. Alternatively, it can go to freeze or numbing out, and you might head to the fridge to finish the carton of ice cream. All of these responses occur in Picasso Response and they continue to place you in dis-stress. This is the time where you say "I am stressed out". This place of feeling completely overwhelmed, is a direct result of living from a sympathetic nervous system stuck in the "on" position from a past trauma.

The first point of awareness that I invite you to take on around distress is to replace this phrase "I am stressed out", with "I am dis-stressed out." By committing to use this new phrasing you are com-mitting to notice when distress is running you. You can then move into your HeartFull Response, and ask yourself some of the follow-ing questions: What exactly is the pattern that is still running? Do I still feel the need to be in control? Do I still feel the need to fix and make better? Do I still feel the need to judge and minimize all others' experiences to feel safe? Do I still need to act confused? There are a multitude of possible patterns that can play out as distress. But all of them are distress and not really stress.

You might have been going into fight, flight or freeze response from the time you were in utero or as a newborn. I have very strong cellular memories from the time I came home from the hospital as a newborn. My middle brother is fifteen months older than I am, and he was very sick as an infant celiac in the 1950s. I remember him crying and I remember feeling very unsafe in a place where a baby could cry and cry with no end in sight. I remember wanting things to simply be calm and end. Flash forward forty years to when my children would cry out of a healthy experience of being disappointed or thwarted: I would experience their crying as my distress. I wanted the crying to end. I wanted to make all their pain and discomfort go away so that I could calm my nervous system down. It was all about me and had nothing to do with my children. I did not have the ability to hold the space for their natural growth and expression of things that were not working for them in their lives. I needed to reframe my view on stress very quickly so that I could allow my children to experience their own lives and the healthy growth that disappointment brings. So that I could be the supportive mother I wanted to be. I needed to go into the wisdom of my heart, find the pattern, acknowledge and release my distress and become present for them. I needed to come out of my own default setting for them, so that they would never need to go into distress themselves. I needed to allow them to learn what healthy stress felt like, knowing that I was there fully and completely for whatever they would experience. Putting this together with what you learned in Chapter 2, "Don't Believe Everything You Think", I needed them to experience healthy stress where they would still have full access to both parts of their brain, rather than distress where they only had access to half their brain. In distress you are lucky if you can access half your brain. Most times it might only be your back, survival brain, that is active.

My invitation to you is to reframe your perspective on stress. You are now in charge of your physical, emotional and spiritual environments. There are no failed environments for you any longer. If your environment or situation is not working for you, you can now move away from it and make healthy choices for yourself. You no longer need to experience dis-stress. Stressful moments are now offering you a new way of becoming aware and relating to yourself—a new way to hear yourself and what you need in the moment. What an amazing adventure you are on.

Invitation

You can probably figure out what I am going to invite you to explore this week. Find your comfy cozy spot—your safe zone. Connect to your inner breath and self and think of a time when you experienced being stressed or as you experienced then, distressed. Now move into the experience with all of your senses, allowing the thoughts and emotions of the experience to come up fully. See what those messengers are telling you right now. Explore if your messenger is a new healthy message or a blast from your past repeating itself and triggering your sympathetic nervous system. Write down any patterns you discover or any new "aha" moments. Check in and make sure that you finish this session by coming back to the safe present moment and to your breath. If you have wandered into your Picasso Response slowly come back through your Aligned Response, to your HeartFull Response, with your grounding cord reaching to the centre of the earth. Thank your body for being such a powerful teacher and giving you this opportunity to develop into your best self. Breathe into your connected holy trinity for five to ten breaths, and then come back to the room and the rest of your day.

CHAPTER 15
The Art of Negativity

THE ENTIRE SOCIETY IS GEARED TO THE NEGATIVE, SKEWED TO THE negative. You look in the newspaper and find mostly negative reporting. You listen to the news and hear disaster after disaster. If you are living from survival you are always looking for the negative space. You ask, what is missing? What is wrong with this picture? What is threatening my future? Seeing what was negative was your survival adaptation. Your ability to see what is negative has become a maladaptation, and will stay one, until you can turn it into a super power. In suffering you are living in the negative. You are the victim and everything bad is happening to you. You are not at "cause" for anything. By surviving you have moved forward out of suffering. But until you can turn negativity into a super power, you will be constantly hyper vigilant for any person, place or thing harbouring potential negativity. You see a person, place or thing as a potential threat, present and looming, even if it is not yet there. You are looking and waiting for danger to appear to you just around the corner. You might even say things like, "I could have hit my head on that", even though you didn't hit your head. There is always a possible threat present in your mind.

If you are a parent you may tend to look at what your kids are not doing well rather than what they are doing well. You look at the dishes left on the counter or the unmade bed and don't look at your child getting up and getting to school on time and attending for six hours of the day. You may be a parent of a child who has challenges or special needs. At first, having you looking for everything that was wrong may have been helpful to their particular therapy. Things that you could report to a doctor or a specialist or a teacher. After awhile the suffering was over and yet you remain hyper vigilant looking for the negative all around and simply surviving the days and moments. If you have a partner and you get stuck in this negative loop, you will tend to look at what your partner forgot to do, or did not think to do rather than all the little things that they did do. You will not be able to see their real expressions of love. If they express their love in a different way than you expect, you will only see lack. You will be missing the exquisite moments that are being gifted to you.

You look at yourself just as negatively. Your hair is not sitting exactly right, or you didn't express yourself properly, or you forgot to pick up the rice for dinner. You see every wrinkle as a failing on your part somehow. You see a lack, a negativity, a missing piece. You miss who you are and how amazing it is that you are actually here, present and accounted for. Rather than looking at all the things that are working in your life and your environment, you see what is not happening or getting done. You gear yourself and your life toward the negative.

This kind of survival impulse is passed down from one generation to another. Most families came to this country from somewhere else. That somewhere else was not necessarily a great place to be, which is why they left. Your family might have undergone racial discrimination, relocation, starvation, rape or a mix of many hardships. The need to look at what was missing in their environment or what was negatively going to impact the family became more important than many of the positive things they could notice. They needed to be on high alert. They needed to measure what might be a risk or a danger and weigh it out quickly and seriously. Their lives and the lives of their children, depended on seeing the negative before it impacted them. The ability to think critically and make decisions based on negative input is what might have allowed them to survive when their neighbours did not. It got them from where they were to where they finally settled. Their suffering might have been over but their need to survive kept running their lives. It became your life as well. It was your survival adaptation until it got in your way of thriving and it became your maladaptation.

There was a study done on rats who are very social animals. They placed half the rats in a control group, the other half were the experimental group. The control group of rats were exposed to a particular smell. The experimental group of rats were exposed to the same smell and were then given an adverse stimulus. Later each set of rats was allowed to breed. The babies from the control group of rats behaved normally in the presence of the smell, but the babies of the experimental group of rats behaved negatively when the smell was first introduced to them even though they had not experienced the adverse stimulus themselves. This survival adaptation lasted for seven generations of baby rats. A very sobering experiment.

In moving away from survival and toward thriving, you will be moving away from a very entrenched habit of seeing the negative and sitting in the fear that lived in all the previous generations of your family. It will be breaking a pattern that not only exists within you, but that you have probably already transferred to your environment and the people within it. You train your kids, your families and your friends just as surely as they train you. You have trained your kids to look around the corner, your partners to see what is missing and your families to never be satisfied. Fear and survival are practices that you have instituted or brought into your life and then rehearsed over and over again. As I mentioned before, our society, news and media also train you to stay in that perpetual place of seeing what is missing from your life and where you are lacking. Retail stores thrive on it, selling you a plethora of products designed to counteract the negatives that you so readily see. But your view of yourself and your world is simply a practice of negativity—not a reality. The glass is only half empty because you have practiced seeing it that way. You know this deep down inside yourself which is why you are here. You are the one to break this cycle and make the shift that will change everything and everyone around you.

Think for a moment. If as studies have shown, you have around sixty-thousand thoughts a day, and forty to fifty-thousand of them are in a repetitive loop of survival thinking, will you easily journey into a state of thriving? Of course not. So then if you are taking the time to practice this art form that we call life and living, why not practice making it a life of a positive reality filled with beauty? Like the art on your wall, choose what feels beautiful and life affirming for your sixty -thousand thoughts. See what is magnificent about you, your children, your partners and your friends. See what is working for you in your work. Notice the wholeness in your mind body and spirit. Do it for yourself and for your loved ones. Do it so you can thrive.

Invitation

For this week I invite you to notice each time you are seeing your glass half empty. See if you can take a moment to look for something that you can see as a half-full glass. When you reframe your thought, you might see it as new reality. Notice not only when you turn towards the negative as your first instinct and notice when those around you are doing it as well. Here is an example of how this could go: you notice that your children didn't bring their plate in to the kitchen from the table. First notice where you are seeing the negative. Do you believe that if they don't take this dish in now they will maintain this pattern in their future? Have you perhaps made this single forgetful act into something greater? Take a moment and be curious about your emotions and thoughts and where they are coming from. Now, can you move away from fear and survival and see a positive somewhere? Perhaps the positive is the fact that you are so lucky that you can all be together eating as a family. Perhaps you are blessed for having all this nutritious food to offer. This does not mean that you can't parent and teach. What it does mean is that when you make that observation, you will be in a totally different place and it will be a neutral and teachable place—not a critical one. Not a place filled with fear and anxiety, teaching and passing down more fear and anxiety. Next look at what you might be saying to yourself about your partner today. Write it down. Look where you can see what is working. What can you enjoy about the moment? Where can you let go of your fears about the future for your loved ones and thrive in the moment? This week is all about becoming aware of what is working about the moment and really enjoying it. Take time to make notes throughout the week on what you noticed and what new practices you are choosing to take on. How does it feel for you to turn towards thriving and away from fear and *survival? Bring that beautiful feeling into your heart as you come into your HeartFull Response. Take ten heart-full breaths here. Teach your body a new way of being. Teach your body the deep feeling of thriving one breath at a time and one celebratory moment at a time.*

CHAPTER 16

Striving Is Not Thriving

THOSE OF YOU WHO HAVE TRUDGED, STEP BY STEP FROM SUFFERING to surviving, may be tempted to believe that you have to work hard to get to thriving. Working hard—or striving—is not thriving. It is more of the same survival action dressed up in a more enlightened outfit. Thriving is a state of being. Be-ing, is a description of your state. Striving, on the other hand is an action, a verb. To strive is to act or do something. To strive is to take the action of reaching beyond your limits or your ability in the moment. You have read all about the maladaptations that you put into place to survive because you did not have the tools at the time of trauma to do anything else. To joyfully skip down the road to thriving, you need to be present. You need to be exactly where you are now. Striving is taking a bit of distress and spicing it up with some judgment, control or perfectionism. It comes out of your mouth as "have to"s, must do"s, or just "got to"s—to name a few. All of these terms immediately take you out of a HeartFull Response or an Aligned Response and place you into your Picasso Response. You have already lived through the consequences of life from this response system.

The old paradigm that you grew up with might have been a paradigm of striving. The paradigm of pushing through and of taking control. Striving is a mind driven strategy. In this strategy you lose access to your emotions as messengers and to your heart as your generator. Staying in this paradigm you lose your connection to your body and your spirit, which is the opposite of what you want to be doing if you are going to be able to thrive and feel alive. Feeling alive does not exist in your mind. It is a body thing, a somatic thing. Your cells tingle, your heart opens, you smile and take full breaths. If you are upset, it only takes a moment for you to connect with your emotion, find your thought, stay in your heart and make a better choice for yourself. Whatever the situation, you are staying present for yourself, allowing yourself the space to move into your HeartFull Response, and living in the moment. You breathe in your heart-full place and release yourself into the next moment with a clean slate and an open heart. When you strive or push through the moment, you shut all your feeling systems down so that you can narrow your focus in the hopes of surviving. You may be striving to survive your "hectic" work schedule or your "emotional" kids or your "demanding" friend. Please note that the adjectives you use to describe your distress could be tied to your stories, which are tied to your surviving. To move in the world from this place is to move in the world disconnected from your inner place of breath, space and heart centre.

You might be saying to yourself, "but I want my children to strive to be the best they can be". Actually—you don't. You want them to step forward into each moment giving their whole selves to the moment. This is the best that anyone can do. Striving works against this. The new paradigm, that I present for you to consider, is one where you step into allowing. You allow your thoughts and emotions to come up, you centre them back into your heart and you simply wait for direction. You take one conscious heart-full breath after another and you listen. It is in this moment of allowing that the authenticity that is you emerges. When you allow yourself to thrive, the striving ends and you feel yourself come alive. You feel the understanding and the wisdom guide you to rise up from inside and expand your options. You and your children can step into a life lived fully.

The other darker side to striving is that it expresses violence and abuse towards self. When you know that you have to go to the washroom and yet you choose to push through to your next stop, you are voluntarily putting your body into distress mode, and doing violence to yourself. Remember Chapter 14, "Distress Or Stress?" You are abusing your body by moving it into the sympathetic nervous system or its fight response. You are fighting yourself. When you say to yourself that you have to read one more chapter or practice one more skill even though you have had a long day, you are pushing and controlling—and you are not allowing. When you have lived through trauma, fighting to survive, striving is second nature. When you strive you feel like you are accomplishing something. Getting down to business and getting things done. Thriving is not that. Being fully alive in yourself in the moment is not that. To thrive you begin to move from having to do your life, to being and allowing your life.

Striving has within it strong components of judgment, control and perfectionism. Taking as an example the situation of needing to go to the bathroom but striving to keep on schedule. In this situation you are making the judgment that the schedule is more important than you and your health, you are controlling your bladder function and you are attempting to be perfect by arriving at your destination right on the button of your agreed time. You are placing the situation above yourself. You are affirming to the world that you, your being and your authentic moment , are not as important as any external persona or situation. You stay on schedule and move to your Picasso Response. You make poor decisions for yourself from this scattered response, and you end up hurting the inside authentic you and those around you. When you finally arrive at your destination you will be acting out of your Picasso Response and everything that flows from there on in your day will have had its seed in your striving. You have literally missed the heart of the situation. You have allowed the striving to move you out of your HeartFull Response and out of a day lived from there.

It is interesting that many traditional prayer practices are about being fully present to what it is that you are praying for. When I worked with a local medicine man he would say "we pray rain, not pray for rain". What he was teaching me was to actually be and feel the thing that you are praying for as if you already had it, or experienced it as your prayer already answered. To pray for health you feel your cells already healthy. You claim it as already demonstrated in your life. You see your children whole and complete. You do this all from a HeartFull Response as, your holy trinity is the only place from which you can experience being and feeling fully in the present moment. This is the place that allows you to generate the energy and send your vibrations out into the world.

When you strive you take yourself out of the present and out of the opportunity of being yourself. You rob yourself of the opportunity to be fully alive in the moment. You rob yourself of your own ability to hear yourself, answer your own needs, and become whole. You disconnect from your ability to be tender, gentle and kind to and for yourself and your family .

In contrast, by staying true to your moment, you are gifting yourself with space. The space for yourself, the space from which you can gift others with your beautiful and authentic self, and the space and opportunity for all to thrive along this path.

Invitation

I invite you to find your cozy, comfy spot. Close your eyes or take a soft focus and come in to your HeartFull Response. Take your time. Without changing the natural depth of your breath, begin to make the breath longer. Lengthen the in breath and lengthen the out breath. Begin to notice the things that are working for you in this moment. It might be your position, or your muscles, or your breath, or the temperature of the room. Simply notice and acknowledge each and every one of the things that is working for you. You might want to say "thank you room temperature for making this time feel delightful", or "thank you joints for allowing my body to be so comfortable". Take your time. You probably spend most of your day on what is not working or going well for you, so this is your time to begin to reverse that energy. You are reversing the energy, changing it, from striving to fix or change something to allowing and thriving in what is open and authentic for you, moment by moment. I invite you to do this as a daily practice this week, preferably in the morning to set up your day but if not try on your lunch break or any other time that will work with ease. You are not striving here, so you will find the time that works gently and easily. It is your time to simply learn to feel what it is like to allow the moment to be in an atmosphere of thriving. It is not a time to shift the body and strive for the perfect position. If your position isn't the thing that is working for you, let it be and simply find those things that are working. Make notes on how this practice changed your experiences on each day that you practiced.

PATH III

Staying The Course

CHAPTER 17

Walking Side by Side

THROUGHOUT THIS BOOK YOU HAVE SEEN HOW TRAUMA LED YOU TO suffering—how suffering was your stepping stone to survival. You've seen how you are now making your way from surviving to thriving. You may have chosen to use the word trauma, or in your own mind, you may have chosen to use words like shock, injury, accident, pain, severe hurt or harm. For the purpose of the rest of your pilgrimage, I will keep to the word trauma. Fill in the word that feels right for you. In my years of experience I have found that you do not get over trauma, or lose it, or talk it out: you don't walk away from it on your HeartFull Way, rather you walk side by side with it. Trauma can be seen, can be recognized and can be felt. You can develop a relationship with trauma, like you would an old but reliable bathrobe, and that relationship remains intact whether you are aware of it or not. Trauma doesn't suddenly disappear out of your life while you are not looking or giving it focus. Trauma lives in your cells and in your cellular memory. The trauma you experienced actually lives in the cells of your body. It lives in the muscles, tissues and organs. When an experience became too overwhelming for your conscious mind, your body in all its wisdom decided to move the memory out of your consciousness and place it in your body. The experience, if it stayed in your conscious mind, would have been so overwhelming, that you would have never survived.

I was once working with a client doing a Dimensional Energy Healing session. She had originally come to me suffering chronic pain. In the middle of the session I received a picture of a room in great detail. Her body's memory was giving me the information that her conscious mind could not. After the session I described everything I saw. She began to cry and let me know that I had just described her Uncle's bedroom in detail. As I worked with her body, the memory of sexual abuse finally re-emerged. At this point and in the presence of safety, her body could release the buried cellular memory into the conscious mind. Slowly, slowly my client and I worked to find a safe relationship with this trauma, so that she could heal the physical pain that she had been holding in her body. You can release much, you can increase awareness and yet the cellular memory of the trauma will live on. It is like a map to what you need to pay attention to and learn to love in yourself and others. It is entirely up to you, to get to know your trauma intimately. It's up to you to get to know how, when and where your trauma lives inside of you. It's up to you to develop a caring relationship with the trauma. To acknowledge yourself, to acknowledge what you have been through, and to be present for the moments that the trauma may still need from you.

The journey is not to get rid of parts of yourselves, the journey is to embrace all parts of yourself, even those that you don't like or would not have chosen. The journey is to have an intimate, loving relationship with all parts of yourself, where you can say, "I know that you are here ready to react, and I thank you for having protected me in the past; I choose for you to settle and I choose to create something new instead". This is your HeartFull Response moment. You may have lived through some violence, and unless you get to know the violence that has been transferred and lives inside you, you may miss it. You may miss the patterns of violence that you are now inflicting on yourself. You may not understand that your pattern of working out in the gym past your limits and sustaining injuries over and over again, is self-inflicted violence. You may not see that judging and shaming yourself and calling yourself names is self-inflicted violence. You may not see that starving yourself in order to become someone that you were not meant to be is self-inflicted violence. When the violence has stopped around you, unless you come into relationship with the trauma, you can internalize the demonizer who simply put, becomes you. By coming into an intimate, trusting and compassionate relationship with the trauma, you can develop the self regulation that you need to move from your Picasso Response to your HeartFull Response, in the moment that you are triggered.

To say that you walk side by side with your trauma, is not to say that once you go through the process of release, the relationship to your trauma will not, potentially be transformed. It will, and you will find the quality of it, very much different. And yet without embracing the relationship as a part of you, the trauma may transform but not transmute. There is a difference. When your trauma transforms, its quality changes. But the trauma stills remains inside the body. When trauma has the opportunity to transmute, it can leave the body and become of you, but no longer part of you. You can be a witness to it as something that once lived inside you, but there is a distance away from you, so you can see it as separate. When you do walk side-by- side with it as an intimate, your trauma becomes like an old familiar shirt that you can choose to put on or not. By practicing coming into your Aligned Response over and over again, and then moving into your HeartFull Response, you give the cellular memory the opportunity to become a whisper and not a scream. You no longer become overwhelmed by the emotions that used to engulf you. You begin to be able to sense the body changes and sensations immediately at the trigger point, the point of stimulus, and you can step to the side rather than stepping in. You no longer go from this trigger point at zero, or no reaction, to a full blown reaction, at one hundred. You do not immediately let the trauma trigger pull you into Picasso Response. There is enough space now and acknowledgment to allow for your journey to your heart. There is a relationship that you can connect with and interface with. You can make choices where there was no space before to do so. By stepping to the side, you walk beside your trauma not constantly through it, so you don't re-experience it. You don't re-traumatize yourself and you don't re-trigger your cells back to survival and fight, flight or freeze.

Within this space and acknowledgment is the ability to move into a place of acceptance. You may not be thrilled with all the parts of yourself and your past experiences and choices, but you can accept them. Acceptance is the pathway that you want to take towards love within your holy trinity. It is one of the most integral parts of this HeartFull Way towards your own sacred ground. As you begin to transform your trauma and then transmute it with the immense love and compassion you are bringing to it, you can begin to see what happened to you as an initiation rather than a type of victimization. Now as an initiate, you get the opportunity to transmute your negative relationship with your trauma into a loving, wise and compassionate relationship. Your particular initiation has taught you a particular wisdom that you can now bring to your life and the lives of others.

I saw my journeys through cancer and the treatments as trials by fire. Being the stubborn learner, I thought that my path was to survive the cancer. I believed at first that all the trauma I felt was new trauma from the experiences of treatment. I then became aware that the trauma that I was experiencing was not new but a re-triggering of all my old traumas around survival. I needed to wake up and step into a relationship with those old traumas so that I could transform them into messengers and transmute them into a loving relationship with myself. As soon as you fracture any part of yourself off from the whole, you minimize yourself. You make yourself less than. You invite judgment and shame. In my case I felt great shame as a healer for getting this cancer not once but three times. Bringing that relationship back to myself allowed me to once again become intimate with my whole self, and to walk side by side with my old trauma and love my whole self fully. I then had the space to thrive rather than simply survive the cancer. Through my initiation I was able to find the wisdom to develop the HeartFull Way program.

You can begin to walk to the side of your trial and beside your trauma by slowly feeling into the parts of you that are OK and the parts of you that hold the pain. You can invite all the fractured parts of yourself back into integration. All the parts of yourself that you chose to discard and leave on the side of the road. Parts that you labelled as needy or inferior or less than. Parts that you were ashamed of, or thought of as weak or broken. A wonderful metaphor for the reintegration of fractured parts is the healing of a broken bone. Most people see a break as something that weakens the bone, something to defend against. But If that bone is set properly, it will heal and become stronger than the bone that never broke. When you come alongside your trauma and don't re-traumatize yourself with judgment, shame and criticism, you are healing yourself stronger than you were before your traumatizing experience. When you walk side by side with your trauma along these lanes and alleys, you can recognize your experience for what it is, recognize your emotions for how they now help you to become intimate with yourself and others, and choose what works in your life and what does not. You will have the acceptance to be able to choose to thrive.

Invitation

I invite you this week to find your cozy, safe place. Take a few breaths to come into your Aligned Response. Then take a few breaths to come into your HeartFull Response. Next bring your awareness and breath deep into your body. When I say this I don't mean taking a deep breath but rather bringing awareness deep into your cells. You are going to begin re-integrating the fractured parts of yourself. You are going to begin this by first finding all the parts of yourself that feel OK. Find a part of you that feels OK in this moment. It may be a toe or a finger. Focus on the feeling of being OK. Stay there for a few breaths really sinking into that feeling of being OK. Now see if you can slowly allow that feeling to spread throughout a little more of your body. Each day begin with the small OK-ness of you and see if by the end of the week you can let this feeling fill your entire being. Notice how you feel at the beginning, in the middle and at the end of this process. Notice at what point you move from OK to a place of pain. Let that place of pain talk to you. Let it share all its experiences and listen to it as you would a good friend. Notice how much of yourself you can re-integrate and reclaim. Remember to take this process very slowly, day by day, centering in your HearFull Response. You can always go back and use your releasing tools at any time. Please end the process in your holy trinity, taking five to ten breaths there. Make notes on your observations throughout the week. Note where you felt OK, where you felt any pain whether that was emotional, physical or spiritual pain and where you built your bridges to re-integration.

CHAPTER 18
Resourcing

IN THE LAST CHAPTER YOU BROUGHT GREATER AWARENESS TO YOUR own experiences of trauma. You stepped into a lifelong relationship with yourself and your own particular pain. You found where you were OK and places that you were not yet OK. Through all of this, you began to create greater space as the trauma moved out of the body for you to witness. You may now have the experience of more and more of your life being OK. You may now be able to focus on more of what is working for you. You may suddenly feel how wonderfully amazing it is to be out walking with your beloved dog around your favourite park instead of needing to dissociate in order to survive the moment. You may be able to release the concept of "have to", "need to" and "must do", from the moment and you may be able to stop looking at it as if it was one more chore. Your moments are bringing you more appreciation. They may also tell you that you are ready to release some memories that you didn't even know were there. As you have read, when you race, you hurry, you dissociate and you numb out, you don't have access to some memories. Those behaviours were your old survival strategies. You are now moving closer and closer to your own thriving. But along the way, the HeartFull Response that you are now practicing, will allow for greater connection to self and therefore greater connection to old memories with new emotional awareness and experience.

This is all exciting. You are coming into a greater relationship with yourself. I like to say that you are coming into a greater relationship with your human life partner, which is you. So how are you going to do all this? How are you going to stay open and experience a deeper connection to yourself when difficult emotions come up? How are you going to stay present to emotions like grief or shame, without reverting back to survival again? Excellent questions and I am so glad that I placed them here. We are going to come up with some resources for you to use during this time of transition—some practices that will assist you in staying your course. These resources will help you externalize your big and old experiences so that you don't have to own them in your present and take them into your future. So let's talk about resourcing as a tool and give you a few examples of how you can use them.

Resources are all around you. You may be using them quite a bit without even realizing that you are doing it. Someone who experiences stress in their work day may decide to come home, change and go for a run in the woods. They feel that the forest and trees that they run amongst literally feeds them and reinvigorates them into aliveness. A forest run like that is a resource. If that same person came home and took the same run, but instead they were thinking about how to get back at their boss the next day. If for the entire time they were running, they did not notice the trees or the flowers or the people they passed by. If they did not allow the moment to feed them, they would be in fight response. A forest run like this is not a place of resource.

If another person came home and got into sweats and got in front of a TV, they would be dissociating. They would be in flight response escaping their day. They would not be coming back into the aliveness of the moment and so that is also not using a resource in the way that I am suggesting it for you. And if yet another person came home after a stressful day and hit the carton of ice cream in the freezer, they would be literally in freeze response, numbing out with food. A real resource, as you want to use it, will bring you out of fight, flight, or freeze response. It will bring you out of your dissociation and your old survival responses, and it will assist you in staying in your HeartFull Response so that you can move back to your path and walk yourself closer to thriving.

Pets, friends, objects and more can be used as resources for you. This way I've developed of using resources with my clients began with needing to find my way through my own triggered nervous system.

As I was on my own HeartFull Way, I suddenly had a memory of when I was a baby and was brought home from the hospital. You already read about my experience hearing my middle brother cry. To compound the situation, my mother went into hospital when I was around six weeks old for surgery. At the time my sensory system was flooded and traumatized. First I suffered the constant crying of my brother and then I suffered the disappearance of my mother. Of course I blamed myself, with my imaginal baby mind, and this blame and shame sat in my unconscious for years. It took my body over fifty years to be in touch with itself enough to release the memory of what I experienced as deep abandonment because of something I perceived I was or something I perceived I had done. I didn't consciously remember the event but as you read about in the last chapter, my cellular memory was holding my emotions and experiences. When I began to find the pain buried within, it came up as a visceral, deep and anguishing fear.

My nervous system was triggered and began to run, because I was reliving a memory from babyhood, from a time when the baby me had nowhere to go and no understanding of what I was experiencing as traumatic fear. As an adult I had this flashback memory and my body would not calm itself, it mimicked the way it was for my original six-week-old self—a six-week-old baby cannot calm itself. You are not born with a parasympathetic or calming, self-regulating nervous system. It is something learned. This triggered nervous system was not going to help me stay in my thriving space.

I took my younger son's first stuffy, and held it, and named it my baby self. I soothed that baby self part of me, telling it, that I, the adult, was here and present and was not going away. I rocked it and spoke to it, assuring it that I was here, I was listening and that I was sorry for all the pain it had experienced. My present day self became the older self, the safe self, the capable self, and my nervous system came back on-line. I was able to witness my present day self as separate from my remembered experience. My past baby self was now separate and embodied in the stuffy, which I could then attend to. I slept with this stuffy, and I let it grow safe and strong and secure under my care. As I moved through other processes on my HeartFull Way, it was this baby self of me, embodied in the stuffy, that would let me know where my nervous system was. My baby self helped me see whether I was in my present adult capable self or acting out as my baby helpless self. To this day I have kept this stuffy in my bed. Now I only return to it as a resource every six or eight months, when I become overwhelmed for a few moments. However, I do make eye contact with it every day, which allows me to always send my love out to those parts of me that I have reclaimed. It allows me to experience present moment love for that part of me that suffered and survived. It allows me to not have to go back into any of those dark places because all of me exists in the light of my present love.

I would like to invite you to consider all the traumatic possibilities that your children might have gone through. I know that once I began unravelling all of this through my own HeartFull Way, I was better able to see the sources of my own children's pain. I was able to help them also find healthy resources to develop the kind of relationships they needed to foster with themselves—without blaming myself for any of this. For instance, my eldest son had a very difficult and long birth. The night he was born they took him away from me and placed him in a nursery for observation. Away from me and as I later came to learn, away from any other babies. The shame that he had buried deep inside his unconscious kept playing out in his life. The shame for being taken away from all human contact—not hearing my voice or any other voices, not feeling or hearing any human breath, not feeling any human contact. He felt great shame coming from his imaginal mind that all of his experiences must be his fault. Somehow he was defective and not worthy of the human community. His need to hide the shame by always going to fight, flight or freeze impacted all his experiences. At first I took on his shame as my shame and blamed myself for the whole mess. Slowly slowly I was able to navigate through my HeartFull Way and focus back on him—coming up with creative resources that we both could use.

In reality of course, many of your early memories are not an accurate depiction of what was happening, but as a baby you could not know that. My brother was very sick and the doctors at the time had no answer. My mother did not develop a strong pelvic floor and as I was the last child my parents were going to have, it made sense to do the surgery after my birth. For my own son, I was put on IVs the night of his birth and they were afraid that he had an infection so needed to monitor his vitals for the night. Your adult selves can come into contact with what seemed overwhelming when you were experiencing it, with the help of a resource like the stuffy.

I learned to find many different resources for myself—and for my children. As I mentioned above I had to come up with creative resources to deal with my son's deep shame. The following is one of the creative resources I discovered for my oldest son, for when he would act out and try to get me to engage with him in his fight response. He would invite me to make him feel small by shutting him down, because his pattern of shame came through as a pattern of unworthiness. I chose instead to stop in my tracks. I would feel my nervous system become agitated and I would feel the need come up to shut him down. I wanted to shut down what was making me feel agitated, which of course was his behaviour bringing me back to a childhood experience of my own. I would not worry in that moment what my own experience had been to trigger this agitation in me. In this moment it was not about me. It was about the pain being experienced by my son. I would choose instead to imagine that I was talking to my father, whom I loved and lost very young. I would easily get into my HeartFull Response from this place and my voice would stay calm, soothing and loving. My son would not be able to push that button. My nervous system would calm and then so would his, and the whole situation would become diffused. Later I could go into my HeartFull Response and find what it was he had triggered inside me and move to release it.

You have a treasure trove of creative resources all around you. As you open to yourself you will come into relationship with various unheard, unanswered parts of yourself. Your ability to externalize them and become the witness by using a symbolic resource, like a stuffy, will be a very powerful tool to keep you present and thriving, so you can stay the course of your pilgrimage. Take time and really explore this invitation so that you construct yourself a hardy toolkit. Please remember that I am always here to contact as well, if you need a human guide through this part of your HeartFull Way.

Invitation

I invite you to find your safe place. Begin to become aware of a time in your life that you relate to as a trauma—a memory that triggers your nervous system to pick up or become agitated. You may want to start with a time that you have been able to walk side -by -side with already so that you can practice this invitation with emotional safety. Think of an object that you have around the house that could represent the you at that age. If you were very little, perhaps a stuffy; if you were a young child perhaps a toy; if the memory comes from your teenage years, perhaps choose a shirt in the style that you wore. Come into your comfy pose and slowly come into your HeartFull Response. For the next few minutes, practice sending love and caring to your object. Tell the object how you are now the adult in charge and how you will keep this "you" aspect safe from any harm. You will be present and all loving. You will hear all the pain and see all the sorrow. Let this aspect of you know that you know the pain it experienced, and let it know how sorry you are. Now feel that and notice if your nervous system is calm. Notice if you can feel the object's "nervous system" as calm. Take a couple of breaths here. Finish by placing your object in a safe place and letting this aspect of you know that you will be there to check in on it and check that it is safe. That place can be in your bed, on a shelf or in a special location you have constructed for this purpose. I invite you this week to check in on your resource every morning and every evening. Check in on your own nervous system and see if you are feeling less triggered by things. Slowly discover what pains you can self- heal with this process. Make whatever notes you like about your experiences. If you have a great handle on this, you can begin to note down all the other resources that you currently use or could begin to use. Really enjoy being creative here. Always begin and end these sessions with your resources in your HeartFull Response, with your grounding cord in place, and take five to ten continuous breaths.

CHAPTER 19
Forgiving

FORGIVING IS NOT SOMETHING THAT YOU DO FOR OTHERS. FORGIVING is something that you do for yourself. You give it to yourself, it's for-giving. You give and you gift yourself. Forgiveness is the practice of moving from the transformation you have experienced with your trauma, to the transmutation of the trauma. Notice that I have changed the language from "your" trauma to "the" trauma. In the last few chapters you have practiced making this shift. You have made the separation from the trauma inhabiting you to walking side by side with it. You are now ready, through forgiveness, to let go of your past and the burdens you so carefully chose to carry—you are ready to gift yourself your present. Your present is your present. Forgiving gives you your future by gifting you with your present moment. Without forgiveness you tie yourself to your past, to your Picasso Response and to staying in surviving: you disable yourself from the authenticity of the moment and thriving.

Without forgiving you will come upon a dead end as you travel into the deeper phases of thriving and self love, which is your destiny. It will hamper your journey to finding your sacred ground. You do not have to accept bad behaviour to enter into forgiving. You do not have to forgive others directly. You do not have to place yourself in any danger, or risk more trauma with your forgiveness. You can begin by forgiving yourself. Forgiving yourself can be the beginning of your forgiveness practice. Forgive yourself for being a part of a situation that involved a trauma to yourself. Forgive yourself for not having known how, or not having had the tools to engage with life as it met you. Forgive yourself for not being present to your own pain until now. Forgive yourself for being too young, too vulnerable, too unaware or too fragile at a particular moment, at a particular time. Forgive yourself for not knowing what the bigger picture was as you were looking through a small lens of judgment or caught in another old pattern.

Self-forgiveness might be where you need to begin. Then to move on forgiving others, you may need to forgive through a surrogate person standing in for the person, or by writing a letter, or by using a symbol. Forgiveness is a practice not a goal, a pathway, not a destination.

You may be able to get in touch with the practice of forgiveness by seeing it in terms of a metaphor like this: if you looked down from another planet at a woman giving birth, not knowing the process, you would see a human being writhing in agony, calling out, sweating and trying to breathe. You would probably see it as an end, a death, an unwanted experience. If you stopped watching then, during labour, you would be left with a very particular story and judgment about humans. You would not have a full picture in order to understand the behaviour or the situation. So it goes with trauma and situations in your lives. You don't have to understand them, just as the interplanetary traveller does not understand human birthing. In your case you also have no way of seeing the end of your journey, and so you may not fully understand your experience. The so-called goals of release and forgiveness are not goals at all but rather part of a journey—your own journey to birth or rebirth.

You began by recognizing emotions, thoughts, stories and patterns around your own particular trauma. You went on to develop an intimate relationship with the various fractured pieces of yourself. You used your resources to see each piece as a part outside yourself. You have transformed the very quality of the trauma. Now you deepen the transmutation to bring these outside pieces back home to yourself. To transmute the trauma through love is to forgive. I know I suggested beginning with forgiving yourself but for some and some situations it may actually be easier to forgive others rather than forgiving yourself. My oldest son taught me a deep lesson around this piece of self -love. Once a year we sit around the table and discuss the process of forgiveness. It was my turn to speak and I said that I found it easier to forgive others than myself. My son asked me to explain further. He must have been sixteen. I said that I found it easy to forgive him for things that he might say or do, but not so easy to forgive myself for giving him a vaccine that caused him to have seizures and have major challenges when he was young. He got up walked over to me and with a great amount of love in his eyes he said, "Oh Mom you have to let that go because I forgive you." Out of the mouth of babes as they say. Forgiveness of self is an expression of your love of self and your commitment to this pilgrimage towards thriving.

Forgiveness of self is not only forgiveness of a manifestation in the physical form, it is a mind, body, and spirit experience. It is forgiveness of the thoughts, of the actions and of the energetic, or what you have been holding in your energetic being. It is part of a deep transmutation of your entire being through this loving practice. It is a practice of letting go of past, present and future so-called mistakes—or as we can now see them, not as mistakes but as moments of not being aligned and in HeartFull Response. Forgiveness is not a fixed state but a moveable and delicious feast to partake of. It is turning complaints about a bill passed in government to a practice of forgiving those who don't know what they don't know. It is an expression of your compassion about being in this human experience. It is a constant opening up into the next moment clear and clean, with nothing from the past being dragged forward, nor fear for the future being pulled in.

If you do not forgive yourself you end up minimizing yourself and then you are in that loop of survival once again. If you are a very creatively expressive person who did not fit in with your peers during high school, and you continue that pattern into adulthood, you will be self sabotaging. As an adult, if you carry that wound, that pattern, of not fitting in, that fractured part of self will make sure that you never express too much, shine too much, stand out too much or arrive at the cutting edge of your field of work and reach the success that you could have reached. The trauma will stay fixed to your experiences. You will not move from transformation to transmutation without forgiveness. You will not be able to move through this next part of your pilgrimage because your lack of forgiveness will bind you to retracing your steps and going back into survival. Forgiveness leads you to transform your trauma to the trauma. Forgiveness leads you to transmute the trauma so it no longer weighs the heart down. To forgive yourself is to free yourself from the past. To forgive others is to gift yourself with the space to experience your real and authentic moments, and open to the thriving future that is ahead of you.

Invitation

This week I invite you on a journey of forgiveness. Find yourself a box, a jar a vase a bowl. Some container that you love and that feels good for you. The container for this is very important. You will want to feel connected to it every time you look at it. I will call this container your heart box. Choose some sticky notes of various colours with enough room to write on. Each different colour will elicit a different feeling inside you so let your creativity express itself here. Not just yellow OK? Notice during the week each time you feel or think of a wound or act out a behaviour that you can identify and name. Then, rather than staying in this place where you might experience self-judgment or shame, come to your safe place with your heart box and sticky notes. Begin by coming into your HeartFull Response, then write down "I forgive myself for...", and place it in your heart box. You can do this every time you find yourself in your Picasso Response acting out or when a memory comes up or when you are triggered in any way. Begin each sticky note with "I forgive myself for..." You can also look back at the past chapters and exercises on emotions, thoughts, stories, and patterns that you may have begun to release and that are now begging for forgiveness. Become aware of anywhere that you are still naming the trauma as my trauma. See if you can bring forgiveness to yourself or to the other or to that experience. Take this journey slowly and enjoy it. Fill up your entire container if you like. Take the steps from transformation to transmutation. Notice how you feel before you write your forgiveness note and notice how you feel after you finish writing your forgiveness note. Write down your self-observations. Remember to always begin by moving into your HeartFull Response and end with your HeartFull Response and ten beautiful breaths. If it ever gets difficult for you, and if you have an object as a resource,

❀

like a stuffy, you can focus your forgiveness by talking to your resource. This process is for you to gift to you. Be loving and gentle with yourself through this entire process.

CHAPTER 20
Gifting Others with Their Journey

ALONG YOUR JOURNEY YOU MAY HAVE BECOME SO HABITUATED TO the stories you tell, the thoughts and emotions you run, the patterns you have practiced and the trauma you have lived, that you find it difficult to let go of them entirely. At first you might even think that you have let them go, but upon taking a closer look you may find they are still showing up within your circle. I say within your circle, as the place they show up is most likely not within your life directly. Rather than give up the pattern entirely you may be living the pattern and dramas vicariously through your friends or family. Remember your dramas could look like sitcoms, mysteries, or action adventures. A pattern can take the form of encouraging your friends to speak about their issues over and over under your "good listener" persona. The move from living your drama to living other peoples' drama is sometimes the bridge that you need to walk on first. Remember too that you have left judgement behind. Letting go of everything that you have practiced faithfully in order to survive can be really foreign at first. The body, in all its wisdom, attracts compensation for the perceived loss of your old faithful pattern, by becoming a magnet for someone to enter into your life who will act out your pattern for you. In this way you get to live it through them but not have it be yours. Except that it is very much yours.

Every pattern carries with it an energetic signature, and as you explored in the first few chapters, a vibrational signature. You may still have a physical addiction to the charge of this known vibrational signature. It is as practiced as the personal signature you write on checks and forms. It has been repeating itself for years. It has given you an illusion of safety for years. It has given you an illusion of protection from experiencing the trauma for years. This energetic vibrational signature, as you read, is usually being transmitted through the frequencies and vibrations of the heart. To change the channel on your heart's radio waves, by changing frequency and vibration, can be both new and unfamiliar. The first few times you choose to make a shift, you may not even feel like yourself. As your HeartFull Response deepens, it can feel very foreign. The self that you were seeks comfort in everything, rather than evolving through what the moment is presenting. The self that you were may choose to go back to the familiar, Picasso Response, now played out by others around you. Being aware when the old pattern begins to attract these old dramas, is the work of your emerging present self.

To explain this need for energetic comfort in terms of your responses, beginning with your Picasso Response—mind to the right, emotions to the left and heart floating somewhere in between. When in the Picasso Response, the energies and vibrations leaving your heart are in your old patterns. They are searching out the old familiar feelings of the trauma. They are searching them out like a tracking beam trying to lock onto its target. You can be in a room with people you don't know and in that need to go back to the familiar, you will lock onto the one or two people who can share something with you that will re-trigger your drama. You need to take a break in the path and take this detour, checking in with yourself. You could be attracting the old feelings of trauma because they are both comfortable and familiar.

Going back through your Aligned Response and then to your HeartFull Response as a daily practice in the presence of others is a vital part of your journey now. It is one thing to be in your holy trinity while on your own and quite another while someone is walking next to you through the forest reciting all too familiar stories and patterns. You take a detour out of your Aligned Response, to notice how you are feeling. You notice how you entered the forest feeling one way and how you are beginning to change while listening to the stories and emotions and patterns of your friend. Are you beginning to resonate with those vibrations? Are they pulling you into your Picasso Response? What does your heart feel like? So you notice, you become aware and you realign your holy trinity right in that very moment, rather than encouraging their drama so that you can get a fix from it. You may want to ask them for five minutes of silent meditative walking. Or you may want to ask to restrict the conversation to a new book that you are both reading. You can shift the moment to give yourself the space to realign and come back to your HeartFull Response that you have been so diligently cultivating—allowing their stories, patterns and dramas not to be part of you any longer. You are not trying to fix, or to change, or to advise or even to listen to them right now. You are not ready yet, or centred in your new vibrational being. You are simply gifting them with the journey they need to take through their own life stories, away from you, so that you can keep the drama out of your space, stay in at least your Aligned Response, if not your HeartFull Response, and move towards thriving.

There is a beautiful story about a man who was working on his car in his driveway. He noticed a butterfly trying desperately to get out of its cocoon. Rather than leaving the butterfly to its own journey, the man, not being able to contain his own patterns, stories, emotions and dramas, interrupted the butterfly's process and helped it out of the cocoon. He was not able to hold the space for the butterfly's struggle. He was not able to separate himself from the struggle. It was too uncomfortable for him to witness. So he swept in to fix the butterfly's problem, and to end his own discomfort. However, by interfering with the journey of the butterfly struggling through the cocoon, the man crippled the butterfly. The struggle of a butterfly to get out of its cocoon, is what spreads the fluid from the cocoon onto the butterfly's wings and thereby allows their wings to take flight. To gift the butterfly with this journey is to allow it to journey towards soaring free.

You are at the stage where you can see your past patterns in others. It is so very easy to want to help them through their struggle and their pain, and to give advice or share what you have learned. Most of the time though, if you are not being asked directly to share what you have learned but are just being drawn into another's drama, you can be sure that it is your vibrations to somehow remain in your pattern that are in control of your life. Take a look at your family dynamics, your friendship dynamics and your work dynamics. Do you see a pattern in any of them? If so make an effort to disengage at the level of trauma and begin to re-engage only on the level of heart. Gifting others with their journey sets everyone free to soar. You are ready to soar. The work you are doing by moving into your HeartFull Response, no matter where you are, is the struggle of the butterfly to get the miraculous flying fluids on its wings. Take the time to gift others with their journey so that your journey becomes a gift.

Invitation

During this week I invite you to notice when you are entering other people's business and not staying on your own path. What sends you over there into their business? Is it your emotions, your stories or the patterns you have with them? Also notice the questions that entice you to get into other people's business. It may be as simple as a baited statement from your friend like, "I just don't know what to do about it anymore"—and off you go into their drama. At this point in your journey I invite you to either gracefully change the subject or allow yourself to be there but be present to yourself first before becoming present to them. See if you can stay externally there while internally practicing your Aligned Response and bringing your pearls into your heart and into HeartFull Response. Then begin to breathe from this heart-full place, completely connected. After several breaths, go back to the external, while staying in this HeartFull Response, noticing if there is any change in what your friend, family member or co-worker is saying. Notice if your shift in energy and vibration changes what is happening. From this place, notice how you can choose to grace your friend with their own life's journey and have it not enter you or shift you from your HeartFull Response. Witness what they are saying and listen to them. You can always say things like "I hear you" or "I understand". Do not do anything more. Notice and become aware of how it feels to be present without having to do anything but stay in your holy trinity. Write down any of the observations you have made and enjoy allowing all the butterflies in your life to find a way to soar for themselves.

CHAPTER 21

Words

ANYONE WHO HAS HEARD STORIES FROM THE BIBLE HAS HEARD THAT the world as we know it was created by words that were spoken. Many other creation stories attest to the power of the word. Whether or not you come from a particular belief or faith, one thing is for certain—words are powerful.

There have been world renowned scientific experiments, done by Masaru Emoto, where words have been placed under a pitcher of water and the molecular structure of the water has changed in direct relation to the word used. Placing a word like, "love" under a pitcher of water has produced more alkaline (read healthier) and sweet-tasting water. Words and energy have been placed with cooked rice. Ann Cosse has put up her experiment on YouTube using Reiki energy with cooked rice. Others have experimented using "hate" thoughts on one container and "love" thoughts on another. The container of rice where "hate" was used spoiled and grew mold and yet the container of rice where the word "love" was used did not. From faith to science, from psychology to literature, your words inform your world. Your words let you know what matters to you and so do they create matter from the thoughts, from the emotions and from the stories that you continue to give voice to.

Most people are very careless with the words they use. You might be one of them. You might be concretizing your experiences without even knowing it. The clearest example that I have for how I concretized my words, or how I moved them from an abstract notion to concrete physical form, was months before I was diagnosed with cancer. I was repeating over and over to myself, "I can't go on like this. I am dead tired." The abstract description of a need for sleep was joined by a powerful emotion of dread and a story of how I could no longer go on in this world—and voila. The abstract became the concrete. The cancer was my way out. Of course in my case it was not, because I was so not ready to leave my children, this world and my work. Words are powerful.

I was speaking recently to a father and daughter about their weekend. When I asked him how his weekend was with his kids he said "the weekend was hard." I asked him if the weekend itself was inherently hard or if some of the experiences he had of the weekend were hard. He replied that it was in fact just one of the experiences. I invited him to change what he was saying to "my experience of having to camp out was hard." He said that out loud. I asked him how he felt and I asked his child how she now felt when her Dad changed up what he was saying. They both said much better. Being specific and clear about your words gives you space to experience other aspects of your life even within an experience of hardship. Using the term "my experience of.." also allowed his children to have their own experiences of the event, as there was not a global feeling being pronounced by their father. Sometimes to keep a close connection with you, your children do not want to contradict what you are saying. All of a sudden a weekend that was full of play and adventure and new experiences gets brought down to its lowest common denominator—in this case the descriptor "hard". Everyone gets on board with using the same words and the possibility of joy and thriving is completely removed.

When you repeat the story that an entire weekend was hard, based on the challenge of one event, you are not only teaching your own body to respond with high stress hormones, you are teaching the bodies of those around you to do the same. You are saying with your globalizing and non specific words, that there were no redeeming moments in the weekend. That there is no room or space for other experiences other than the whole and entirety of the weekend being hard. You send everyone into fighting the experience, fleeing from the experience or numbing out from the experience. I know as parents you would never purposefully create memories like that. Take a moment to let this idea land for you. How often do you think you have globalized one moment's experience into an entire day? By repeating the negative moment over and over and reliving it with your words, how might you be changing the molecular structure of the water that mostly makes up your body? How would you be influencing all those around you?

Neuroscience tells us that neurons that fire together wire together. If you are not discreetly using your words, you can continue to fire and wire your neurons and nervous system to see the world in black and white, safe or unsafe, friendly or threatening. The more you strengthen these neural pathways, the more you tell your body that this life that you are living is all or nothing. Hard or easy, bad or good. If just one thing in your entire weekend was hard and you keep repeating that the whole weekend was hard and focussing on those words, you are reinforcing the neural pathways of your Picasso Response. However, if you can get more specific, more precise and more discreet about your words you can stop pulling yourself back into a Picasso Response, stop bringing yourself back to survival mode. By changing your language, you stay on your journey, begin to make the space for your Aligned Response, take the breaths needed to centre in your HeartFull Response, build the bridge of regulated neural pathways, and open up your entrance to thriving in the moment.

The other piece to being unclear about your words, is that our bodies react or respond to our words. Words will not only reinforce certain neural pathways they will also program recurring behaviours. These programs will send a message to the brain to prune, to wither and to get rid of alternate pathways as you are no longer using them. Pruning is part of the brain's function. If for example, you learned a language when you were a child and then never spoke it again for fifteen years, the brain would prune the neural pathways related to that language. Remember—neurons that fire together wire together, and neurons that no longer fire, get pruned. Using words that create and recreate global feelings of threat will wire together and entrench those behavioural patterns and chemical responses. Your ability to easily calm yourself or take the space to come into your Aligned Response and move to your HeartFull Response will be pruned away. You will experience drama after drama in your life. You will try course after course and still not be able to move into your thriving place. You will wonder why this is happening to you and perhaps even slide back to your place of suffering for a time. This is not the experience that you so desire to have. Therefore, you must take responsibility for getting clear with your words. Catch yourself when you recognize that you are retelling stories that re-traumatize you and those around you. Take the time to restructure your sentences like the way positive words restructured the water and the rice in the examples at the beginning of the chapter. This is not to say that you won't have negative experiences, but the idea is to isolate them as moments that were experienced. Moments where you heard yourself, received yourself and your messages and then moved on into your HeartFull Response and your thriving path.

You have probably heard the story about how women who live together in the same house have their cycles at the same time. The same goes for families who live in the same house. Not only are your own neural pathways affected by your words, but your language is contributing to wiring your children's and your partner's neural pathways as well. It is your choice whether these pathways continue to be strengthened, in stress and trauma or in calm and ease. It is up to you whether your family's path veers back to surviving the moment, or whether it moves forward thriving into the moment. Use words that will help to isolate more traumatic events in your day and free up the brain to create new pathways to more calming responses, more alive responses and more thriving in your life.

Invitation

I invite you to use your words very specifically this week. This week will be all about becoming aware. To help you become that aware witness, I suggest that you connect into your Aligned Response and then move into your HeartFull Response, breathing there for three to five breaths every hour if possible. It will be like taking mini breaks in your day. Then when a triggering moment enters your life see if you can choose to isolate it in time and space by saying "my experience of this was..." rather than globalizing the event from a moment to a whole day or longer. Play with what words serve you and help you to isolate these triggering events into the smallest spaces of your day. Notice the difference when you choose to retell the event in this new way as compared to how you might have retold it before. See how the change in the words that you use makes you feel. Take a few minutes to write down your experiences this week. You might even notice with the repeated movement to Aligned Response and then to your HeartFull Response with continuous breathing, that you no longer have any desire to use your precious words to retell these types of past events other than to acknowledge yourself for no longer allowing them to re-traumatize you. You might find that you are now using your words to describe all the thriving experiences that you are having and the moments that have you feeling fully alive and engaged with your life.

CHAPTER 22

The World Around You

IN THE PAST YOU EXPERIENCED MORE BREAKDOWNS THAN BREAK-throughs. You looked to the personal and you reacted out of your Picasso Response. How very far you have come. Step by step and inch by inch your HeartFull Response has become your default response.

So why in the face of everything you now know is there still these possible experiences of breakdowns? The first thing to consider is physics. Yes, physics—like how you can see a bright, shiny star in the sky even though it has already died out. What you see is the light that has already passed. When you holler into a canyon, the voice that reaches back at you has already been spoken. Both the light and the voice are echoes back from time. Current challenges are not always related to what you are doing now, but rather what you were doing before, finishing their final echoes or passes through your life The so called, "breakdown", that you see in your environment today is an echo of the voice that you called out with in your past. You have now seen the power of your patterns, your words, and your choices. In your past environment, you did not have the tools to come into your HeartFull Response. Your heart was sending vibrations or radio waves out from your Picasso Response. Sometimes there is a delay in these vibrations coming back to you. Sometimes they take longer to reverberate back and so you have a breakdown without knowing why it is happening. Perhaps you were once dealing with a physical pain: perhaps that pain has now left your body because you have become aware of all the thoughts, emotions, stories and patterns that were stuck. It could be that a few months go by with you feeling great, and then out of nowhere you get triggered, you move back to your Picasso Response and you re-experience your pain. If you have been playing with the past chapter invitations the breakdown that you are currently experiencing in your body is not a "failure to thrive". It is the body telling you that it is ready to look a little deeper, perhaps walk back through some of the lanes and paths you have already tread on. Your breakdown is your body telling you that you sent something from yourself into your environment and that it is returning back to you for greater examination. It might have been a replayed story, thought, emotion or pattern—something so like a comfortable and familiar bathrobe, that you hadn't even noticed that you were doing it. Or it might be something that makes you go, "aha, right, I remember now. I said this over and over again just last month". I invite you to completely remove the idea of "failure to thrive" from your belief system, and know that having breakdowns is part of staying on your HeartFull Way.

How do you know the difference between past reverberations and current vibrations? If your environment is bringing you experiences that you quickly adjust to or learn from, they are echoes of the past. You have already shifted and can adjust and make healthy choices as the adult in charge. As this adult you can stay in HeartFull Response or move back into it as quickly as you used to move into Picasso Response. This is the adult you that is in full and complete service to your best interests and is now taking gentle and kind care of you.

Here is an example of the process I went through, when a triggered physical pain, came up once again from the past. This was an experience of past reverberations, not of a current vibration. In the past I had run stories of not being supported. These were stories that came from childhood experiences of loss. I also experienced pain from the past trauma in my right hip. I moved through these experiences, and I began to walk side by side with the trauma that stimulated them. The pain in my right hip was gone. Then a friend of mine asked me to send out an email about her new course to my data base. I happily said yes to support her, and sent her new workshop offering out to my groups. I then had an emotion that came up for me. My ninety second messenger told me to pay attention to my own need for support. I noticed that over time she had never sent out my monthly newsletters or my class information to her network. Heeding my messenger I decided that the next time registration was open for my classes I would request that she send out my newsletter to her data base. I sent it out to her with a memo to please forward. I did not get any clear reply so I asked directly if she had sent it out. At that point I received an email from her that she was sending out her own emails to her group and did not want to send any more out right then. All of a sudden the pain in my hip came back. In the past I would have taken this "failure to thrive" or breakdown in my environment to be both a reflection on her (an example of my judgment), and a reflection on me (an example of personalizing the situation). The thoughts would go something like, "she is not a good friend: I am there for her and she is not there for me. This is a one-sided relationship..." On and on. The emotions would have gone to: "I feel hurt, disappointed, discouraged, disheartened..." The patterns would have gone to not being heard or seen, or to not mattering enough, or to being betrayed. The patterns would gather more energy and get more entrenched, and if I wanted to squash things down and get back to feeling good again, I would experience non-stop pain again in my physical body. Instead, when this breakdown showed up I immediately went into my HeartFull Response. I took my ten breaths and noticed what showed up as I looked over my past few months. I remembered clearly how one month prior to this event, I shared "war" stories about my children when they were young. I had relived the emotions and thoughts of not being supported. I was not clear with the way I spoke and used my words, and I didn't isolate the experiences. They had inched their way back into my being and I had continued to vibrate them out through my heart. I went back and did a complete release and forgiving for myself. My breath was at ease and I felt no Picasso Response. I realized that this was a faint echo from my past and simply moved on with grace and empathy in my heart. This was not a "failure to thrive". My pain was gone that night. Do you know what happened the next day? That friend of mine emailed me and said she was able to now send out my email. My heart vibration had shifted and the world around me did as well.

An environmental or situational breakdown is not you or all your well earned gains breaking down. Sometimes it will take awhile to recognize what is going on. Sometimes you will have to put a very strong boundary in place in order to get the distance and space you need to process within this part of your discovery. Sometimes you might even have to stop seeing a friend, or end a friendship that was formed in a past reverberation and continues to live within it. Sometimes it will take a few moments and sometimes it will take a few months. These are very important steps to take on your HeartFull Way. If you see your past echoing in your future and really let that knowingness centre into your heart, you will understand that your present choices will become your tomorrow's echoes. What do you want these echoes to be? Do you want abusive situations to follow you? Do you want narcissistic relationships to flourish around you? Do you want dysfunctional thoughts to guide you? Or do you want the echoes of empathy, compassion, connection and respect to be your future experiences? These are now your choices to make. These are now your opportunities to take. You are now your very own adult in charge and you are the one and only parent on duty. It is your turn to create the most wonderful you and the most wonderful environment for that wonderful you. It is your turn to actually create the world that surrounds you on this journey.

Invitation

Once long ago I was at a poetry reading of Rumi, the Sufi poet. He wrote a poem about how we are the bees and our bodies the honeycomb. How our intention builds the body cell by cell, not the body first and our intention next—or at least this is how I understood it at the time. So we will go with this concept for the purpose of this week's invitation. I invite you to see yourself creating your body cell by cell through this healing practice. Please practice this new healing tool for yourself anytime you feel inspired to create your new body. I invite you to find your safe, comfy and centring place. Connect to your breath in your body and move to find your breath within your HeartFull Response. Notice if your breathing changes when it is centred within your holy trinity. Take your time. Come into the self inside your skin. Once you can feel yourself inside your skin, begin to imagine that another, energetic "you" floats away and comes to face you. You now have your inhabited body you, on one side and your spirit body you, in front. Allow yourselves to smile at each other, hold each other's hands and get to know one another. Take your time. When it feels right your spirit body will ask your inhabited body if it can place its hands on your head or shoulders and begin an energetic healing. I invite you to say yes and allow your spirit body to do a loving healing. Take as much time as you like here. Feel your cells renewing themselves one at a time. When you feel complete let your spirit body know. You may choose to celebrate this healing together by holding hands, embracing, jumping up and down on the bed, or dancing. Whatever will bring joy to you. Then come back to your breath and reintegrate your spirit body you, knowing that it is always available to you and that this healing is too. Take your time to breathe in this integration within your HeartFull Response and releasing your grounding cord to the centre of the earth. Once you feel centred and grounded *again you can come back to the room and your writing. I invite you to write down how you felt during this experience. Notice what you might be feeling or sensing after this healing.*

⊕

CHAPTER 23
Boundaries

IN THE FILM THE GODFATHER, ONE OF THE MOST FAMOUS AND MOST often repeated lines is when Al Pacino says that every time he thinks that he has gotten out, they pull him back in. That is probably kind of what you might be feeling now. You probably feel like you are doing all this work to get clear, to lose the stories, to walk side by side with the trauma, and that you have achieved a measure of calm. You have chosen to gift others with their own journeys and focus on your words. Everything is moving along more quickly for you and you find yourself in your HeartFull Response more and more. You feel like you are coming closer to the heart of thriving. And then it happens. You get pulled back into someone else's stuff or a past trauma in disguise, and you are re-triggered and right back in Picasso Response. Not only are you right back experiencing the old traumas, but you are feeling worse than you felt before. Your nervous system is taking it worse than before. The good news is that it feels worse now because you have been feeling so much better. Remember what you read on pruning in Chapter 21, "Words"? You have successfully pruned the neural pathway leading to feeling in distress, and have rewired your body to default to your HeatFull Response. Now going into your Picasso Response feels more unfamiliar and less your normal way of being in the world. It works kind of like when you detox. When you clean up your body you become more sensitive to the crappy food out there compared to the people who are eating it on a daily basis. This is all good news, although it might take you a bit to acknowledge it as such.

Another way to look at this is to see yourself like an enclosed system. Perhaps you can imagine yourself as an egg. Everything that is happening to you is happening within your egg. It is all very personal and while you were surviving you identified with it all. You became what was going on inside your egg. You might want to go back to Chapter 11, "It Isn't Personal" to remind yourself of this part of the road that you have tread upon. So now you emerge as the chick outside the egg. You begin to tease out all the various parts like your stories, thoughts, emotions and patterns. They are being removed from your inner egg and they can be seen as something apart from you just as you are now outside of the egg that contained them. You gain perspective through distance. You can witness your shifts and make use of your super powers. You are no longer an egg holding all the trauma inside. You have begun to release and create space as the chick. You begin to see the other chicks out in the world and also the other eggs. The people who have released and are really thriving and those who are in their egg holding on for dear life, surviving. Without judging any of them—you left judgement behind—you notice that you are attracted to some and not so to others.

When this shift in view happens life begins to slow down. You see the exact things that held you to surviving played out in others around you. It is apart from you and yet you still have cords connecting you to these energetic patterns or vibrations of your past experiences. It is these cords that, without your conscious wish, are drawing people with similar experiences back into your life, even when you don't feel attracted to them. You may already have them in your family, living with you, because as we have seen in previous chapters, as you created your super powers, you created a working survival system and part of that was training the people around you in a very unconscious way. This is where the *Godfather* line comes in. You feel drawn right back into it. The problem is, now it is making you frustrated or angry and yet you don't know how to make it stop which makes you more frustrated and angrier. First, understand that this is a natural part of the process and take a breath. Like any cords they begin somewhere and end somewhere. A cord that ties up a ship begins on the ship and ends on the dock. Sometimes you are the ship and sometimes you are the dock. I say this because sometimes the cord will originate from you and sometimes it will originate from another person who is moving from surviving to thriving, going through the same journey as you are. Do you need to figure all this out in the moment? No you don't. That would be crazy making for you. What helps is to keep this metaphor in the back of your mind while you are pulled into your Picasso Response. If the cord is originating from you and you are the ship, you simply become aware of the experience that is still very much alive in your cells. To best respond to this awareness, you may need to go back to Chapter 9, " Release", Chapter 19, "Forgiving" or Chapter 17, "Walking Side By Side". Take the time you need to come into relationship with this lingering piece, and from your HeartFull Response make decisions that are now life affirming for yourself. With the tools that you now have, the anger is only a messenger who has come to tell you that there is more to discover. With acknowledgment of the message and taking the steps to come into a deep relationship to what the message is here to reveal to you, your anger will come in and go out like any wave might against the hull of your ship. No need for it to stay bumping you around.

However, if you discover that you are the dock and the cord is originating from someone else, becoming aware as quickly as possible allows you the space you need to create clear boundaries for yourself around that particular person and that particular situation. Healthy boundaries in this situation, will allow that baby chick in you to continue to grow and thrive. Not having boundaries in your past might have helped you to develop some super power like becoming empathic. Being an empath would have worked in your favour if you needed to know what a volatile caregiver was feeling so you could avoid their rage. It could also have helped if you had a child that was experiencing a disability and could not express themself. When there is no boundary between you and those around you, you can feel into other people's needs more easily. Now being empathic is your super power and you can choose to use it when you need to. It is time for you to develop and nurture your own healthy boundaries, so that you no longer need to be hyper vigilant, and protect yourself from other people's energies—so you can avoid starting the whole survival cycle again.

You will begin with using boundaries as a tool while you are still vulnerable on this very new journey of yours. Your boundaries are not for the purpose of separating you from or placing you above others. Your boundaries will begin from your HeartFull Response so that you can now move from witnessing yourself to also witnessing others without becoming part of their experiences. Boundaries will allow you to continue to gift them with their own paths and choose the people and experiences that will nurture you, feed you and bring you to a life lived fully. So where to start setting boundaries? You start at this week's invitation.

Invitation

This week I invite you to begin with your *Aligned Response.*
Now move into your *HeartFull Response.* Bring your mind
body and your emotional body into your heart and take three
long breaths there. When you feel very centred in your holy
trinity imagine your favourite colour. Imagine this colour in
you and all around you. What does that feel like for you? Feel
how that allows the energy through your heart to expand. Let
this feeling vibrate in through your heart. Let's call this feeling
your "Yes". It might be a beautiful blue which makes you feel
calm or a vibrant green which makes you feel connected to life.
Take the time to find your colour, its feeling and your "Yes".
Now let's find the opposite. Imagine your last argument with
someone you loved—and stay in your HeartFull Response for
this. It will be hard to do because you will immediately see how
your mind is going one way, how your emotions are going the
other way and how your heart is completely abandoned. You
are now in your Picasso Response. The Picasso Response is your
"No". In this place you might now feel your heart rate picking up
and your nervous system begin to buzz. In your "No" you have
moved again towards surviving and it no longer feels well to
you. This is a marvellous place to have moved to. Remember
that in survival your "No" is always running so you never
before noticed the difference. You are now becoming a thriver
and that allows you to feel this difference.

This week when you begin to feel your own Picasso
Response, notice what is happening around you. This is where
your first boundary gets placed. It might be small. One example
of positive boundary setting from my own life came about
when one of my sons was a teenager. When he got home from
school the first thing he would do was "dump" all his stuff from
his day on me. I would immediately want to solve things—

problem solving is my super power—and so I would go into fight response and solve mode. The first boundary I set was by making the request that when he comes home he take five minutes where he reconnects to himself in his space after which time he is invited to tell me everything. Of course, the result was huge and my relationship to myself and to him grew exponentially. I was no longer the leader-parent and became the supporter-parent I wanted to be. I was longer his trash bin but was his confidante. His ability to self soothe grew exponentially. Start with just one boundary for this week. Notice and allow your nervous system to begin to feel the beautiful experience of taking gentle and attentive care of yourself, instead of falling into your Picasso Response. Make any notes on what really worked for you this week and on how it made you feel.

Boundaries

PATH IV

Finding Sacred Ground

CHAPTER 24
Connection

YOU HAVE COME TO THE POINT OF THE HEARTFULL WAY THAT WILL reveal your very own personal sacred ground. You are about to find what is holy and sacred in you and in this pilgrimage. It is not a journey routed in knowledge but one that is rooted in wisdom. The type of wisdom I speak of here is one of transcendence.

You have transformed your trauma by stepping into an intimate awareness of your patterns and by finding your super powers through those patterns. You have transmuted the traumas with your practice of forgiving. You have been able to walk the pilgrimage through your deep commitment to your HeartFull Response. You are now treading on the path to transcendence. You are transcending from the knowledge of self that you discovered in the first three parts of this book into the deep wisdom of thriving. Connection will be your first stepping stone on these final paths. It is the wisdom of connection that lives in your HeartFull Response, your holy trinity. It is a wisdom that does not need to see "connection" as one particular thing or another. For some it can be a connection to love, for some the quantum field, and for some they may prefer God. The connection to something more than yourself is all that is required.

In utero, your first developing stem cells are that of the heart and tongue. What a perfect world your body is. I believe that this order of development is not a simple accident of your physiology. The tongue connects you to self expression and the heart connects you to a vast vibrational field of possibility. Both together create the connections that are greater than the self alone. The ancient Greeks believed that the gods needed humans to pray so that they would know what to do. They believed that a human prayer was the tongue speaking the heart's desires and this was the direction that the gods should take on behalf of a person. Prayer has many negative overtones for people. You might have your own personal connection to prayer or be completely adverse to the word. Just for this week, I would like to invite you to suspend any personal or religious ties to the word and see the word prayer as synonymous with connection—your connection to your own private thriving life: your connection to a field of infinite possibility: your connection to actually guiding this energy and light within from your holy trinity.

This week I invite you to play with the connection that comes from the HeartFull Response that you have been practicing, combined with a prayer of purpose that comes from your tongue. You will be speaking this prayer of purpose out loud. Speaking a prayer of purpose is speaking a direction to your heart. You are directing your heart's vibration on a very specific frequency. You are taking the radio wave frequency that you learned about in earlier chapters and guiding it in service to yourself and others.

Many programs speak about using an affirmation. You may have seen movies and read books that focussed on affirmations. I know that in my yoga teacher training, affirmation was part of the philosophical focus. But an affirmation is more like a head thing, a mind thing, a decision that you are making for yourself. A prayer of purpose is a heart thing, a feeling, a vibration and an invitation. Let's say you are going to a party and you are single. You may create an affirmation about meeting that special person for your self at the party. This would be setting a "mind" goal. It is very specific, targeted and narrow. A prayer of purpose is different. In this same situation it is saying that you wish to feel a sense of belonging at the party. Or that you wish to feel magical moments at the party. Unlike an affirmation, there is no exact outcome or goal. A prayer of purpose is a feeling that your heart can understand and resonate, a vibration that then goes outward before you. When I have worked with my clients in this model they report completely different results. When they have gone to a party with an affirmation about meeting someone and they haven't met anyone, they have reported coming home depressed and unhappy. However, when I invited them to go to their next party with a heart-full prayer of purpose feeling a sense of belonging they have come back reporting that they felt great because all these connections happened within the sense they had of feeling that they "belonged". Did they meet their next relationship? No they did not. But they were at the party and they were thriving—and if there would be a chance to meet someone and have it be a positive meeting the best way to do that would be thriving in possibility, attracting people to your beautiful light. With the feelings of this prayer of purpose resonating from your heart, you are now standing on sacred ground.

Sometimes you may feel so out of alignment that you can't connect to your prayer of purpose. In those moments when you are in your Picasso Response, notice what your mind is saying or what emotions you are having. Your prayer of purpose will lie in the opposite of that. If you are experiencing emotions of loneliness then belonging would work as a prayer of purpose. If you are thinking that there is no hope for you, then inviting the possibility of wonder and surprise would work. If you are noticing lack in your life then your prayer of purpose would be about wholeness. If you started in your Picasso Response, come back through your Aligned Response and then go into you HeartFull Response to create your prayer of purpose. Creating a prayer of purpose is a vibrationally potent practice, and you want it to be coming from a centred heart place.

When you use your mind to create an affirmation, your mind is looking at you as a separate identity—not as a connected being. There is an "I" in the centre of your mind's story. Your mind can gear its affirmations very specifically toward outcomes that aren't connected to anything greater than yourself. For example, I can create an affirmation for my book. I can say, "I see my book selling in the top bookstores in North America". In contrast to that affirmation, see how a prayer of purpose works. When you use your heart to create a prayer of purpose, you feel connected to something greater than just you. From my heart, I can say "I commit to being a contribution to the lives of others." Can you feel the difference between the two approaches? The affirmation is finite and the prayer of purpose is infinite. The affirmation is what I would call a closed system and the prayer of purpose is an open system of possibility.

Take a moment to close your eyes and move into you HeartFull Response. See if you can play with this concept. Perhaps consider an affirmation with your finances. Notice the difference between saying "I see myself making $*****.00 this month", as compared with a prayer of purpose saying "Money is flowing freely and easily to me from any and all sources". Breathing into your holy trinity, become peaceful and connected. Notice how it feels to be in this miraculous place of connection creating your very own prayer of purpose. See if you can become connected to that creative field of all and infinite possibility. That field of thriving.

Learning to work with a prayer of purpose rather than an affirmation is a practice of connection. You have been using your HeartFull Response to uncover and get to know so much through the book this far. You are now invited to use that holy trinity to generate the vibrations that create the life you want to live. Take a moment to make your connection to your heart and to notice your life's purpose revealed there. You need not see the words "life's purpose" to mean your entire life: rather your life in this moment. For some of you it may now be easy to see life's purpose and for others, noticing where you are now will begin to open that access point. Your ability to thrive lies in your ability to connect to your heart and its prayer of purpose on a moment to moment basis and to speak it out loud. Celebrate this connection and your ability to create a life fully lived. The gods are listening.

Invitation

I invite you to find your comfy safe place. The best time to do the following practice would be the morning, but you can choose the time that will work best for you. Notice the quality of your breath. Line up your mind, heart and belly—your Aligned Response. Now slowly merge them together within your HeartFull Response and begin your continuous breathing. Enjoy your holy trinity and take a moment to notice the colour of your HeartFull Response today. For the next week, as you breathe into your HeartFull Response, invite access to your heart and to your prayer of purpose for the day. One day your prayer of purpose might be "feeling your connections", another day it might be "feeling your spark of creativity or inspiration". Whatever it is, your prayer of purpose leads you to experience yourself in real time. Take at least ten breaths here and then recite your prayer of purpose out loud so that you can hear it with your own ears. Make a note below of what your daily prayer of purpose was. Or, if you would like, as I mentioned in the Introduction, you can use a lovely journal, and write down your prayer of purpose for your day one page at a time. Remember to write your prayer of purpose down only after you have said it out loud. The purpose of the journal is to invite yourself to continue writing down your prayer of purpose on a daily basis well past this one week invitation. Play, celebrate and thrive through this week. Write down what was easy for you and what was more challenging. Write down how you felt for the day and what you observed happening. At the end of your week read all your various notes. Notice if there has been a shift in your heart feelings around the things that you wrote down. If your prayer of purpose was to feel your sparks of inspiration—are you noticing more of them through this practice and in your days activities? If your prayer of purpose was to

🏵️

experience more acceptance—are you finding more moments of acceptance for yourself? Explore the impact of deeply connecting to yourself daily with your prayer of purpose.

_____

_____

_____

_____

_____

_____

_____

_____

_____

_____

_____

_____

_____

_____

_____

_____

_____

_____

_____

_____

_____

_____

_____

_____

_____

_____

_____

_____

_____

_____

_____

_____

_____

_____

_____

_____

❁

CHAPTER 25
Expansion

YOU HAVE JUST STEPPED INTO CONNECTION. YOU ARE BEGINNING TO transcend yourself. You are one of many small parts of this Universe. Scientists say that the Universe is ever expanding. They speak about how the Universe is expanding outwards. As a part of the whole Universe, you are expanding outwards.

If you look at the word Universe you see that it translates to "one verse", from the Latin "unus"—one, and "versus"—line of poetry or song. You are ever expanding—one verse at a time. Your heart is the centre from which you expand outwards. Your heart creates the vibrations that you generate one verse at a time. Your one verse comes from your connection to your prayer of purpose and your heart produces the expansion to create your new life of thriving.

When you take a moment to study what you are in reality, you will see atoms that are filled with a whole lot of space and moving energy. When you use the heart and your heart's brain to centre and generate this energy, rather than the mind or the belly, in Picasso Response, you get to guide that energy and make it completely expansive and coherent in your Universe. When you work with your heart, the who that you think you are no longer exists, rather you find you are becoming the what of all. You shift from a thought or an emotion to an actual state of feeling or being. You are no longer thinking about ease, or emoting calm, because you are now being peace. There is a vibrational connection and expansion that transcends you and feels like the peace that exists everywhere in the Universe.

Now, I know you have heard the saying that "we are all one". This can be a hard concept to relate to. It can be a challenge to allow it to land deeply inside. Perhaps the way to look at it, is not to take the perspective that we are all one and the same, but rather to take the perspective that our heart's are one and the same. Our heart's are all the one and same generators. No matter where you live on this globe, the heart is your mechanism by which you expand and generate the frequencies that create your unique world. When you can feel into this heart truth, you can invite the resonance of expansion. Of course I am not the same as a person who has grown up across the world under completely different circumstances than I have. I am not the same as you are. But what we all share is the same desires that emanate from the heart. You are magnetized just the same as I am, as the earth is and as are all the beings and creatures that exist here. The Universe actually lives in you, and you live in the Universe. You generate both positive and negative energies just as every living being does, whether it is a person, animal or plant. The sun produces positive ions the rain negative ones. Your heart produces from a place of either a HeartFull Response or a Picasso Response. A positive response or a negative response.

You have already learned the ninety second rule of emotions. You have seen what happens when you compound your emotions with stories and repeat your patterns over and over again on the same day, week, month or onwards. At this part of your journey, your heart is now living the new you that you have worked very hard to transform and transmute. The you that has transformed all these negative energies into positive frequencies. I once heard Wayne Dyer speak about thoughts. Putting what he said into my own words here, "if you were to choose your outfit for the day would you choose an ugly one or the one you believed to be lovely?" If you were to choose your home environment, would you choose ugly colours and decor or would you choose what you felt was beautiful? So the question that begs for your answer is, if you were to choose your thoughts for the day, which would you choose? Would you choose ugly thoughts or those full of joy and grace? You have been playing with these exact concepts. In fact, you have already expanded this concept to your thoughts, emotions, patterns and super powers. It is now time to really get the impact of your transmutation, and make the final choices for yourself. Will you choose to create ugly or will you choose to create lovely experiences? Will you choose to create negative or will you choose to create positive relationships? Whatever you choose will expand out from your heart into your entire Universe.

To paraphrase Einstein, you can't solve the problem within the same energy that created it. You have been exploring the energies of self in the present and now you are approaching the energies of transcendence. This is a completely different energy—an energy of simply being in the now. I invite you to choose this new vibration of expansion. A completely different energy and one that has the potential to shift your Universe.

When I'm working with expansion, I have the image of a white lace butterfly that leaves from my heart and expands outward. If I am in my Picasso Response and so am not choosing a vibration that will serve me well, that graceful white lace butterfly leaves my heart and on the way out, coloured by my Picasso Response, it turns into a hornet. And that is what the world receives. Not my white lace butterfly but my stinging hornet. It is not my intention to do this, as you now know, it is my lack of presence with myself. When I am not aware of myself, my now honed and powerful heart sends out the hornet and the outcomes are not what I would like to experience. When I am choosing well for myself, and I am in my HeartFull Response with a powerful prayer of purpose for my day, then the white lace butterfly leaves my heart and is received by other hearts as a white lace butterfly. Now magic and infinite possibility become my experience. My Universe expands.

Cultivating compassion is another aspect of being in expansion. When you live through compassion you begin to understand the lack of understanding that exists within the world you inhabit. Through cultivating this simple understanding you move into a state of grace, which is a state of being, not of doing. You can expand out as a what, as a state of being, and then send forth your white lace butterfly. When you expand out butterfly-to-butterfly rather than person-to-person, magic happens. You are no longer projecting out of self. You are relating out of a state of one-verse. You are being one-verse. I encourage you to use a symbol for your one-verse as it makes it easier to transcend the self that is you. I have experienced miracles with my clients when they work from a symbol. One of my clients worked as a social worker with young people suffering under poverty and addictions. She was encountering many challenges while trying to create relationships with her clients. As soon as she was able to transcend the self that she was projecting, and find her own symbol to generate, she could meet her clients in a whole different Universe. They could no longer see her as the who that she was projecting before—the who of white, middle class, educated, woman, etc. She was now an expansion of her one -verse out to the world, and with that they could become vulnerable. The same goes for when you approach your children as their Mom, a who, compared to a vibration of love, a what. Using a symbol for being in a state of love will allow you to generate that heart vibration and coherence more quickly and easily.

It is now your time to choose. You can continue to spend time doing, or you can relax, kick back, do less and simply focus on being. Find your symbol and generate your one-verse. When you choose to expand from your being you actually find that you do less—that there is less for you to do. You don't focus on anything that needs fixing or changing. You don't focus on anything that you are missing. You actually focus on a state of beautiful being and expansion happens from there. It has to happen, because you are an expansive Universe unto yourself. This is your one-verse, your authentic verse. Live it fully.

Invitation

Gently come into your safe comfy space and then move into your HeartFull Response. By now I am sure you have your one best way of doing this. Before you can expand I invite you to check in and see what is up for you. Whatever it is, spend some time accepting it and being OK to begin from there. Come into your holy trinity, send your grounding cord in place and allow your breath to release anything that is not working for you in this moment—anything that is preventing you from staying in a HeartFull Response and in your heart. Breathe it out down your grounding cord. Give yourself time here. When you feel a sense of emptiness in that space where you have released, it is time to begin creating. I am going to invite you to create the image or symbol that will work best for you, from your heart. Create your version of my white lace butterfly. This can be any image or symbol. It can be a dove, or an orchid, or...? It can be white, or purple, or...? Explore play and connect with your symbol of expansion. Once you have it clear in your heart, begin by sending it out like a radio wave frequency. Observe what happens within your immediate surroundings. Bring this practice with you on a walk in a park, in the forest, at your place of work, in your bed as you go to sleep and as you wake up. Notice if your beloved symbol changes to something else—like my hornet—depending on whether or not you are staying clear present and in your HeartFull Response. Perhaps your symbol begins as one object and then you get into a dis-agreement with your child. What is it now? Is it even there, or has it shifted and changed? Observe and write down anything you have experience while practising this during the week. Enjoy your expansion into the authentic expression of your one-verse—your Universe.

CHAPTER 26
Self-love

IN ONE OF RUMI'S POEMS, HE SPEAKS TO THE FOLLOWING CONCEPT: IF you could only see who you really are you would bow to yourself. I believe that if you could only see who you really are you would love yourself, fully and completely. If you could really look at yourself as a spirit first and foremost, having a human experience on an earthly plane and so see yourself in a sense like an alien might, you would have much compassion. By compassion, I mean understanding that you are a pure spirit walking amidst the muck and mire of this human experience. Being human is an experience where we confront infinite possibilities of pain on this human playing field until we remember who it is we truly are, spirit. If you can transcend out of the self into the spirit of you, you can begin to connect to that love of self. When you can meet yourself in your heart, you can meet yourself in love of self—you allow your thoughts and emotions to be in conversation with your heart. You grace yourself with all the gifts that exist within the conversation taking place within your holy trinity of mind, belly and heart. You don't stop the thoughts or emotions moving into your heart, or spiritualize them before you give them a voice and a chance for this vital self-conversation. You allow the love of your heart to be the support for your thoughts and for your emotions—their support, their loving lens and their navigator. You move into the true you that is part of the divine state of being in wholeness. You begin to feel that the divine is a complete state of being in self love.

To move into self-love is to move into self-compassion. Your pilgrimage up to now, brought you in touch with all the fractured pieces of yourself. You have connected to yourself and to what is greater than you. You have learned ways to expand out from the heart in love and now this love, brings the compassion back to you and integrates your whole Universe. Having compassion, you understand your own lack of understanding. Moving into self-love, means you do not have to dig into the depths of that which you do not understand—the darkness that no longer serves you. Self-love simply invites you to raise yourself up in the vibration of love. It allows you the understanding that you do not understand and that you do not need to understand. You can stop needing to do so much. You do not need to understand why someone did what they did. Self-love recognizes that you love yourself enough to let go of needing to understand. Self-love recognizes your need for self-conversation, self-integration and then finally self- recognition. Unless you give yourself the time to go through this journey toward and within your heart, you will simply accept the love that you think you deserve. And how is that working for you?

I have so many clients who adore their pets, lavish attention on their plants and gardens, spend time caring tenderly for the earth and yet never do the same for themselves. It is as if these clients are acting from a place that they don't deserve the same kinds of adoration, acknowledgment and love. And yet they and you, are spirit come to this planet.

Recently I had a client who was devastated, believing herself to be overweight without any option of shifting her physical state. I was very clear with her that losing weight was a very real and viable goal but that I found through experience, was not a useful starting point. We spoke more in-depth from a mind, body, spirit platform, and somewhere in the conversation we landed on her cat. "My beautiful, exquisite twelve-year-old cat who, by the way, is slightly overweight but deserves it at her age," were her exact words. A very interesting statement in light of her feelings about her own body and what she came to my office to "fix". Now consider this in light of my previous statement—that you accept the love you feel you deserve. My beautiful, exquisite forty-three-year-old client—who, by the way, "was slightly overweight", did not believe that she deserved anyone's love.

She did not love herself, but rather judged and tried to control herself to reach her perfect weight. She was at the beginning of the HeartFull Way. Her trauma was internalized. So we took the journey together all the way to this point of self-love. It was here that the work really blossomed for her—and weight naturally came off. It was here that she could gift herself with all the love that she had previously sent out in her prayer of purpose. It was here in the place of ultimate self-compassion that the love that she sent out could now reverberate back to her. Here her heart was not only open to generate outward but also to receive completely. A tree that does not receive carbon dioxide cannot give off oxygen. Just as a flower or a tree must both give out and receive so must you. Being receptive is your access point to self-love. Within that wisdom is your path for self-love.

Within the depths of your HeartFull Response to expand and to receive, is the path to your thriving. This is especially true for children who have lived through trauma. Their path to being able to receive their own self-love has been blocked. Once you learn how to love yourself, you are able to remove the boulders and stones in the way of your children. Once you learn the skills for yourself, you are able to model behaviour and help them navigate the detours. Because of many of my early life traumas I too was looking outside of myself for acknowledgment. The moment I could tread on the stepping stones of self-love, much changed for me. The moment that I could grant myself my own right to exist, my heart stayed open and available to generate a life of thriving.

Once you get to this place of thriving self-love, the love you continue to grow is built on your connection and your ability to expand. Look at this as a flow, or as part of an infinity sign, which symbolizes your infinite capacity for self-love. Imagine the infinity sign, a figure 8 turned on its side. When working with connection and expansion, you reach in to connect with your heart and then you reach out and you expand. Expanding sends the love back to your heart to connect into it again, and so there is more self-love to expand out with, and on it goes. Forwards and backwards it goes, creating infinite expansion and loving possibilities. The possibility to love and to be in love with yourself and your life.

Love allows you to be part of everything. Love allows for that security and oneness to occur. It is where you can meet your true self in this human experience. It is where you can attract more loving by being in love with your true self—by believing yourself to be deserving you have your own approval and you come from self-love. You love yourself enough to let go of things that don't enliven you, grow you or expand you. You love yourself, so you tell yourself loving things every day, when you get up, or look in the mirror, or put your clothes on, or prepare your food. All these moments are daily opportunities to display self-love. You can say to yourself, "I love you, I keep you safe, I see you, I am here for you, I care for you, I move you through these delicious poses, I cook for you". Let your body hear your own loving statements throughout your day. Teach your children this practice.

You don't need to like every way you chose to behave in singular moments, you simply allow yourself to love it all. It's like your children. You don't need to like all their various wacky behaviours, you just love them, as they say, warts and all. You can love your anxiety or your indecision or your weight. You can love yourself in the midst of health challenges or emotional challenges. You can love yourself for being courageous enough to take on these different experiences. You recognize yourself in the midst of this human existence as infinitely loveable. Self-love allows you to make good choices for yourself and it will allow your children to do the same no matter where they are. Self-love is knowing in your entire being that your very existence in the world is more than enough. It is a blessing. You are that blessing.

Love is a verb. Self-love is an action in your heart. When you stay committed to being in your holy trinity—thoughts, emotions and heart—when you stay committed to being in your HeartFull Response, your gift is self-love. Self-love will ask you, "what do you feel and what do you need in any given moment?" Your responses to the questions are your own demonstrations of self-love. Self-love allows you to be filled with a true feeling of thriving. It gives you an inner sanctuary where you know that you are part of this life and yet not of it. Self love informs your heart that you are home and you are calling forth your time for thriving.

Invitation

I invite you to come into your safe place. The place that you have created for yourself through this HeartFull Way is a place where you can be secure. It is a place where you have already let yourself be open and vulnerable. Take a moment, breathe and find this place for yourself. Find the breath. Notice its quality, its rhythm—your rhythm. Allow yourself to come into your HeartFull Response. Feel the connection to you and the expansion of yourself. Ask the question, "What would I love here in this moment?" Trust the answer. Allow yourself to experience the feelings as if you have already received the answer to your own question. Let everything else that you thought that you needed to have, fall away. Simply be in the feelings of having your answer fulfilled. If, for example, you ask and the answer is that you would like a life partner, feel what that would feel like to have. Perhaps acknowledge where you might already have life partners in this moment. Perhaps your life partner is a pet or a dear friend. Feel the power and the strength in that partnership. Feel the connection and the love in having your yearning already heard and answered. Take a moment to feel this grace. If you happen to ask and the answer is "a new job", feel what that new job would feel like and understand that your question has already been answered from inside of you. Take a moment here to feel your own creative force. The creation of this idea and the feeling it brings is already the beginning of having a new job. Notice how granting your own requests feels. Notice how listening to your own prayer of purpose and one-verse feels. Take five to ten breaths here. Then slowly begin to come back to the room, to your body and to movement. I invite you to write down the different answers and responses that you experienced with this exercise over the week. Each time you ask yourself the question "What would I love here in this moment?"

🙏

you will receive a different answer, as each time you ask is a new moment. Sometimes the moment is so full and beautiful you might notice that your answer is "nothing more than this feeling of self -love". Notice and enjoy that loving feeling as well. Be in love with yourself.

Self-love

CHAPTER 27
Trust

EINSTEIN SAID, "THE MOST IMPORTANT QUESTION YOU COULD EVER ask, is if the Universe is a friendly place". For you this is the ultimate point of transcendence. For someone who has lived through trauma it is the ultimate leap of faith. To have gone through trauma is to have experienced your world as unsafe. You have now walked a beautiful pilgrimage, and you are at the point of where you are generating your own self-love. There is no consistent self-love without trust. Trust that indeed this Universe is a friendly place. Without trust it is impossible to thrive.

I am not asking you here to have blind faith. I am inviting you to look at the HeartFull Way that you have been treading upon, see what it is that you have been able to create and trust in it. You are on a journey you call life. You know and have experienced all kinds of things crossing your path and bubbling up to the surface of your being. You have become a witness to all parts of yourself and you have moved from surviving to your threshold of thriving. Yet you may still encounter situations where your new found trust in yourself, in your connections, in your ability to expand and to create, will get challenged. Where your ingrained lack of trust from your early life experiences, wants to take hold of you once more. This is where you centre in even more on your own self-love. This is where you realize the wisdom of your inherent loving nature and that of the Universe you are creating and thriving into even more. Losing trust will erode this stepping stone towards thriving. So let's look at a couple of possibilities that can happen in your life.

You may experience an unexpected death in the family that seems to bear no resemblance to a positive outcome. "How could it?", you say to yourself. But perhaps the death was to show you that you could never lose this person—that they are always there for you. You may find that the person can be even closer to you out of physical form. You may find that they can be your guide, and actually be with you constantly. They may be closer and more "on call" than they were when you had to chase them down in their physical form. That kind of trust and faith in the kind, loving nature of the Universe you are creating will allow you to greet these challenging experiences knowing they are there for you to grow your own capacity for thriving. In the situation mentioned above, perhaps you needed a guide on the other side to help you continue to thrive. Trust helps to inform your perspective into one that supports you to thrive.

Or perhaps you find your self still sick. Perhaps your ongoing illness is your vehicle to locate your intuitive abilities. Because you need to stay still through this illness, you have the opportunity of developing this more intuitive part of yourself. You are given the time and space to do that. You are being given the opportunity to test your trust and centre very deeply in that awareness, which is a deep access point for intuition.

Going through chemotherapy treatments a number of times, I was given the gift of a huge shift in my ability to trust my own healing process. I was given this insight into trust by my dearest friend who works at Manitoba Cancer Care. I was on the phone with her sharing my experience of feeling deep fatigue due to the ongoing therapy I was receiving. I was losing trust and faith in my choices. She heard me and then replied, "Of course you feel like that. Your beautiful body is working hard to make all these sparkling, new healthy cells." A light-bulb went off for me at that moment. Usually you are told how your therapy is killing cancer cells. Members of the alternative health community go even further and tell you how the therapy is not only killing cancer cells but also killing you and your healthy cells. Every time you feel tired you end up thinking about all the killing that is being done in your body. This shift to trusting my body and its process celebrated the creative force alive and well inside me rather than the killing and death. Every time I felt tired I was able to say to myself, " Good for you. You are making all these new sparkly healthy Tinkerbell cells." Even on days where I couldn't do more than lie around I felt like I was accomplishing much as I rebuilt my body with brand new healthy cells. I felt like a success. I felt like life. I felt rejuvenated and regenerated. I felt trust in my body again, and with it a connection to expansion, self-love and thriving.

Trust means you are not allowing your experiences to dictate your reality. In other words, the experience is saying one thing but you are not allowing this to define who you are or what your authentic process of life and thriving is. You trust that these two things are very separate and simply co-exist at the same time in our small understanding of the time- space continuum. You don't negate your experiences but you realign and come back into your HeartFull Response, and you centre in feelings of connection, trust, expansion and love. These feelings that carry with them a vibration to co-create something completely different than the energy that was used to create the so called negative experience in the first place.

Sometimes you will have done a lot of growing and shifting and all of a sudden something shows up that side swipes you and takes you for a loop. You can't imagine why it is happening and your hard won trust seems to slip by you. Please remember what you read about echoes of the past showing up in your present. It is not something from your present reality. It is a ghost from the past—an echo reverberating in your present. I invite you to separate from it and allow the ghost to be transformed and transmuted by your present heart energy and reality. Let yourself transcend to the new place that you are standing in—the present place, one stepping stone away from thriving. Stay in trust and move past this last stepping stone. Move from the small picture of what seems to be happening to the big picture of trusting what is truly happening.

When I was journeying through cancer I needed to make a choice. I could either choose to stay in the experience of the cancer or I could step out of that skin and be in a greater reality, a universal authentic reality of connection, growth, self-love, health and trust. Was it difficult? Of course it was. I am a human being not some other type of being. As a human I loved my stories even if I said that I didn't. I loved my emotions even if I said that I didn't. And I loved my patterns even if I said that I didn't. I was a very strong creator and kept creating the cancer. I needed to find the trust that I was, exactly where I needed to be. That what was happening to me was what needed to happen. That I was safe and healthy no matter what was showing up in the current reality of my life. I needed to trust that I could thrive in the middle of all of it and not fear for mere survival because I was being held, taken care of and loved by something so much greater than my small understanding of what existed. Did I follow medical advice? Absolutely. But I knew that those procedures would not work without my ability to trust in both processes of healing—internal and external, physical and energetic, matter and spirit, my earth world and the world of the Universe.

I have clients who are desperately looking for their soulmate or their life partner. They have emotions of loneliness and they have stories of defeat. I invite them to look through the perspective of trust. Trust that what they really need to be doing for themselves at this time, may need to happen with them out of a relationship. Trust that they are being asked to embrace a greater type of relationship first and foremost, a relationship with themselves and the co-creative forces of expansion. Trust that they will be OK and that something will show up that they never expected out of this place of connection and trust. Trust that they have no idea yet of how this will all play out.

Your life is not what seems to be happening. Your life is divine guidance being expressed through and around you. Your life is your ability to trust that guidance, to trust that you are safe, to trust that you are heard, trust that you are held in love and trust that you are here to thrive. I invite you to feel what this last statement feels like in your heart. Trust that thriving is your inalienable right. Trust that thriving is your one true verse. I invite you to trust it, vibrate with it and let it be felt deep within your bones. You are now available to thrive.

Invitation

I invite you to come into your safe, trusting place. The place that you have created for yourself thus far. Come into your holy trinity. This is a place where you have already found trust. It is a place where you have already let yourself be open and vulnerable. Take a moment to simply breathe. Notice your breath. Do you trust your breath to come in and out, to bring oxygen in and to release carbon dioxide out? Notice if you can feel this trust. Do you trust your breath to bring you nourishment on the in breath and release waste on the out breath? Notice if you can feel this trust. Can you trust your life in the same way? Can you trust your life to bring you in contact with what experiences will serve you and to release that which no longer serves you? Notice. If you hold your breath too long what happens? If you hold on to an emotion, thought or story too long, what happens? If you hold on to an experience too long, what happens? Can you trust life to bring you what is needed? Can you trust your breath, your life, yourself? Take a few minutes now to breathe into this very intimate place within yourself. When you feel complete, slowly come back to your physical senses by wiggling your feet and hands. Open your eyes and write down what you experienced, heard or saw in this invitation.

_____

_____

_____

_____

_____

_____

_____

The HeartFull Way

CHAPTER 28

Thriving

YOU ARE HERE BECAUSE YOU ARE READY. YOU HAVE BUMPED UP against your full, overwhelmed life and are now standing in your new way of being in your world, the HeartFull Way. You have put down the armour you wore in surviving and taken on the opening, connectedness and vulnerability of thriving. You are willing to see less as more and vulnerability as strength. You have just walked, step by step, on your own HeartFull Way. As on any journey, you may have stubbed your toe, blistered your heel or become fatigued. But you kept going and now, step by step, you have come to the threshold of your new life. You have completed this pilgrimage and you are ready to thrive. You are ready to live a life filled with infinite possibility and wholeness. A life of thriving.

You have released your past, are sitting deeply connected in your present and can now dance your way into your future You have transformed, transmuted and transcended the pain and trauma. You have moved path by path to this exact time and place in your life. You are a HeartFull being. Take a breath and feel your ease and peace. If you listen you will hear this whisper of thriving everywhere in your life. You will hear it on the inside, in the beating of your own heart, in the growth of your hair, or in waking up after a night's sleep. You will hear it on the outside, in the wagging tail of your dog, or the complete trust of your sleeping child, or the blooming, year after year, of the tulips in your garden. The key to thriving is your simple ability to centre in this deep universal wisdom—centre in this recognition of yourself, in your connection, expansion, trust and love, in every moment and with all your being. When you see your child smile and really notice his presence with your presence, you have responded to this whisper of your life's thriving—this whisper that says, "Look at me, I am your mirror. I am life's creation like you. And like you I am responding, growing and blossoming through the gift of the presence you are providing for me."

To thrive is to recognize that exactly where you are in every moment, there exists infinite possibility and love. To thrive is to recognize the expression of this in all of your life. To thrive is to experience a life filled with contribution, connection, creativity and abundance. It is a life animated by your HeartFull Response. It is your life animated by inner passion and light. It is a life force that burns brightly, as a reflection of your deep wisdom. It is the HeartFull you that allows you to go to the heart of the moment despite what your human experience is showing you. And if you stay centred there for long enough, in your holy trinity, you will thrive as you release your human experience into contribution, connection, creativity and abundance. You will thrive—as to thrive is your very birthright.

When you can centre and feel this thriving birthright there is no more need for "wake-up" calls. There is no more need for experiences where you feel hopeless and helpless. This HeartFull Way has not been easy for me. I have been a really hard nut. I have had to experience not one cancer, but three. It has been far easier for me to fall back on my fears—surviving, rather than making thriving my go-to position. I have allowed worry to be the easier place to land rather than the recognition of trust in this friendly and loving Universe. I now call on this trust. I am not help-less, I am fully supported. I am not hope-less. I choose to be present to the moment and choose not be taken to a future that does not yet exist. I am a thriver and so now are you. Thriving is neither about hope for what you want nor about worry for what might happen. Thriving invites you to create your life from the all-loving HeartFull Response that provides the guidance for you on all levels.

Truly thriving is the ability to hold the space for yourself and others to expand and grow. When thriving you hold the space for your family and your children to experience themselves living fully. Truly thriving is living your moment fully, enjoying every type of experience, knowing that you are now the grown up and this is not going to take you down. You are now the parent on duty and you will be present for yourself on all levels. You are available to be your own witness, noticing all the various sensations that you are going through during any given experience, and recognizing them as your very own human experience. To thrive is to recognize that you are not on this path alone. To thrive is to recognize your vibration, to recognize that you are vibrating particles, part of all the other vibrating particles, which are part of this friendly Universe you call home. To thrive is to recognize yourself as a powerful and beautiful heart being. What wouldn't you do for your heart, and what wouldn't your heart do for you? To thrive is to recognize the infinite potential and possibility that you are—separately and together; to recognize the many vibrations that you are capable of being. The choice to be a fast or slow vibration, a low or high -pitched vibration, a soft or loud vibration or a lowering or rising vibration— the all-loving infinite self vibration of you.

A client of mine recently went for a job interview. As she was describing her experience to me and fretting about what the outcome might be I invited her to take a pause. I next invited her to lock on to the vibration of the person that interviewed her. I invited my client to vibrate in a creative coherent pitch from her HeartFull Response, connecting to the person and expanding out with love and trust in the outcome. After a few minutes I asked my client how she felt. She said she felt at peace and at ease. She said she felt wonderful, clear and empowered. I suggested that she repeat this exercise morning and night until she heard back about the job she was applying for. Two weeks later I got an ecstatic voicemail saying that she got the job, and more importantly that this deep profound wisdom of The HeartFull Way, and the thriving it led to, had landed for her.

To thrive is to notice your vibrations on all the levels that make up you. Become aware of yourself as a mental, physical, emotional and spiritual being. Do not fracture or banish any of these parts of yourself. Rather than making any of these parts less than another, you embrace and hold dear each of the parts, knowing that they are your human experience. They are each worthy of your time and they each bring gifts to your thriving life. Become aware of how you feed each of these parts of yourself—how you take care and provide for each of these parts of yourself. When you nurture all these parts equally you are giving guidance to the gods. You are expressing your prayer of purpose. You are demonstrating through all your various activities and your related vibrations what thriving looks like for you. You are communicating intimately with yourself. Quality sleep, great food, loving people around, creative ideas, HeartFull Response practice, appreciation and gratitude are the vibrations you want to share with yourself, with your children, with your family and friends, and in your life. You are providing all the space for thriving in your life. It is like a pebble in a pond, expanding out in larger and larger circles. For each moment you gift yourself with thriving you are creating many more moments of thriving. You are continually giving yourself the opportunity to vibrate in response to your very own thriving resonance.

You are here because you are ready. You are ready to live your life fully and in the HeartFull Way. You have found your scared ground and you are ready to thrive.

Invitation

I would like to invite you to bring your heart box for this invitation. Place your heart box in the area that you have created, your safe and quiet place. Leave sticky notes and a pen next to the box. Throughout this week, every time you recognize some whisper of thriving, some experience that you are having that is part of the new thriving that is you, write it down and place it in your box. Instead of describing the experience, notice the feeling and write that down. For example if your daughter ran up and gave you a "kiss for nothing", you might write "I am affection". If someone let you go ahead in a line-up you might write, "I am appreciation". If you notice a beautiful flower that just pushed its way through the soil you can write "I am radiant". The possibilities are infinite. Hold your sticky note close to your heart and take a few breaths into your HeartFull Response before placing your gift inside your heart box. Enjoy and play and may you thrive moment to moment, day by day and year by year.

POSTSCRIPT

I would like to take this opportunity to thank you for the honour of being your guide on this, your HeartFull Way. Before I go any further I would like to also offer you a bonus practice—a practice that helped to keep me in my HeartFull Response while going through my own travels. This practice allowed me to centre in my heart while experiencing the various challenges it took to raise my children; a practice that really allowed me to see my experiences with my children as a gift; a practice that helped to keep me out of my mind and emotions and in touch with the moment. This practice also allowed me to keep my faith when being told that the outcome for the cancer I had was very bleak. I offer it here as a talisman to carry with you while you are going through your own journey—for the moments where you feel exceptionally vulnerable to what is going on around you. This practice is quick and easy and can be done in under five minutes at any time during your day. There are many types of practice that I offer to my clients for their use at different points during The HeartFull Way. I did not want to end this book without gifting you this most lovely one. It is a combination of the Ho'oponopono Prayer (from Hawaii) and a hand mudra (or pose). This practice helps to join both sides of the body, hold them in a loving place, and move you out of fight, flight or freeze response, into your parasympathetic nervous system and into an experience of deep connection. Staying in this state for two to three minutes allows the brain an opportunity to rewire itself and come to HeartFull Response as your new, thriving default response.

I invite you to clasp your hands together in front of your heart space. This is not prayer pose but an actual holding of your hands. Beginning in prayer pose, interweave your fingers so that the right is holding the left, and the left is holding the right. This pose joins both hemispheres of your brain together. Place your hands in your lap or in front of your heart space in the centre of your chest. Move into your HeartFull Response, set your grounding cord in place and take five continuous breaths there. Now you can move into the prayer itself. There are four verses and I will describe each one in a few different ways.

I am sorry
Please forgive me
Thank you
I love you

This can be interpreted as if you are speaking directly to your heart. "I am sorry for forgetting my HeartFull Response. Please forgive me for forgetting my HeartFull Response. Thank you for forgiving me. I love you and feel this divine connection to all." You may repeat the I love you over and over again feeling deeply into your heart. I suggest that you say it at least three times: "I love you, I love you, I love you." You can also use this prayer when you act out of your Picasso Response and snap at your child. You can say, "I am sorry for not seeing the pain in my child, please forgive me for not seeing the pain in my child, thank you for forgiving me and I love you and I love my child." Repeat "I love you and I love my child" three times here. You can also interpret this prayer as, "I am sorry for forgetting that I am connected to something greater than myself, please forgive me for forgetting my connection, thank you for this forgiveness and grace, I love you and am connected to you." Again repeat "I love you" three times. Keep your hands clasped together at your heart space for a few more breaths after finishing your last "I love you". Know that you can practice this as many times in your day that feels right for you. You can also move into this practice even if you are having a challenge moving out of Picasso Response. The whole practice is designed to help you move into HeartFull Response at the most trying of times and to settle the entire body down, taking it out of any fight, flight or freeze response. Enjoy playing with this practice and making it your own.

People travel on a holy pilgrimage every year, at every transition or whenever the spirit moves them. I would like to invite you to see The HeartFull Way within this context. I myself walk these beautiful paths and roads on a yearly basis. Every time I discover something more;

another stone to turn, another alley to explore, another lane to walk down. Know that this book is a lifelong resource for you, wherever your journey takes you. We as humans have many layers. Sometimes your first pilgrimage goes through most of these layers and sometimes it does not. For some of you, it might take the whole HeartFull Way to integrate just one layer. Then, when you walk these paths again, you zoom right through all your layers. Each time you embark on this journey you do so as a new person in a new moment. I am always delighted to be of service to you at anytime during your travels; whenever you come up against a blind alley or if you wish to discover new, unmarked routes.

Ask yourself what the impact would be on your entire life if you could stay connected, expansive, vulnerable, loving and thriving all the way through the next fifty years. I know what amazing possibilities are in store for you when you are able to thrive fully. I have seen the animation of my clients' lives and I can't wait for you to experience that kind of joy, health and vitality. I can't wait for you to continue to practice and become a shining light from the inside out. I can't wait for you to live your life fully.

Sometimes you will be able to take The HeartFull Way on your own and sometimes you may need a guide. My desire is to assist you, as your guide on this journey of animating every part of your life. Of guiding you from surviving to thriving. Below you will find my contact information. Please feel free to connect with me for a private HeartFull Way session. This may be done in person, via Skype or on the phone. You may reach out for assistance in creating a book practice class or discussion circles. Know that you are not now, nor will you ever be, alone on this journey.

From my heart to yours,

Sarina Auriel
sarinaauriel@gmail.com
www.auriel.ca

63948818R00140

Made in the USA
Charleston, SC
16 November 2016